It was only a matter of time before a clever publisher realized that there is an audience for whom *Exile on Main Street* or *Electric Ladyland* are as significant and worthy of study as *The Catcher in the Rye* or *Middlemarch* ... The series ... is freewheeling and eclectic, ranging from minute rock-geek analysis to idiosyncratic personal celebration — *The New York Times Book Review*

Ideal for the rock geek who thinks liner notes just aren't enough — *Rolling Stone*

One of the coolest publishing imprints on the planet — *Bookslut*

These are for the insane collectors out there who appreciate fantastic design, well-executed thinking, and things that make your house look cool. Each volume in this series takes a seminal album and breaks it down in startling minutiae. We love these. We are huge nerds — *Vice*

A brilliant series ... each one a work of real love — *NME* (UK)

Passionate, obsessive, and smart — *Nylon*

Religious tracts for the rock 'n' roll faithful — *Boldtype*

[A] consistently excellent series — *Uncut* (UK)

We ... aren't naive enough to think that we're your only source for reading about music (but if we had our way ... watch out). For those of you who really like to know everything there is to know about an album, you'd do well to check out Continuum's "33 1/3" series of books — *Pitchfork*

For reviews of individual titles in the series, please visit our blog at 333sound.com and our website at http://www.bloomsbury.com/musicandsoundstudies

Follow us on Twitter: @333books

Like us on Facebook: https://www.facebook.com/33.3books

For a complete list of books in this series, see the back of this book

For more information about the series, please visit our new blog:

www.333sound.com

Where you'll find:

– Author and artist interviews

– Author profiles

– News about the series

– How to submit a proposal to our open call

– Things we find amusing

Murmur

33⅓

J. Niimi

BLOOMSBURY ACADEMIC
NEW YORK · LONDON · OXFORD · NEW DELHI · SYDNEY

BLOOMSBURY ACADEMIC
Bloomsbury Publishing Inc
1385 Broadway, New York, NY 10018, USA
50 Bedford Square, London, WC1B 3DP, UK
29 Earlsfort Terrace, Dublin 2, Ireland

BLOOMSBURY, BLOOMSBURY ACADEMIC and the Diana logo are
trademarks of Bloomsbury Publishing Plc

First published in 2005 by the Continuum International Publishing
Group Inc
Reprinted by Bloomsbury Academic 2013, 2014, 2015, 2017, 2018 (twice), 2020 (three times)

Niimi, J.
Murmur/J. Niimi.
p. cm. – (33 1/3)
ISBN: 0-8264-1672-1 (pbk.: alk. paper)
1. R.E.M. (Musical group). Murmur.
2. R.E.M. (Musical group)
I. Title. II. Series.
ML421.R22N55 2005
782.42166'092'2—dc22

ISBN: PB: 978-0-8264-1672-8
ePDF: 978-1-4411-5273-2
ePUB: 978-1-4411-8152-7

Series: 33 1/3, volume 22

Printed and bound in Great Britain

To find out more about our authors and books visit www.bloomsbury.
com and sign up for our newsletters.

CONTENTS

ACKNOWLEDGMENTS

Many thanks go out to Don Dixon and Mitch Easter, who graciously took time out from the business of shaping American pop music to accommodate me when I induced them to sit on their laurels for a minute. I'm grateful for their intelligence, honesty, and generosity. I also want to thank my friend Seth Sanders, who used to write about rock music but then got bored, and, looking into his boredom the way he used to look into rock, he now writes about God exclusively. Then there's Mike O'Flaherty, who continually makes me think he could write a better book about almost any idea I come up with, which instead of making me hate him, makes him the most valuable friend anyone could hope to have—thanks, Mike, for all your amazing help. I would also like to thank my editor, David Barker, for his enthusiasm and editorial aplomb, and Gabriella Page-Fort at Continuum. Last but not least, thanks go out to Jay Williams at *Critical Inquiry* for helping iron out portions of the book, Robert Muhlbock for supplying crucial research materials, Andy Creighton for his crafty ears, my cohorts at the University of Chicago

Library for their patience and understanding, and Melissa Maerz for her ongoing encouragement. And finally, a warm thanks to my family, who have always been there for me through thick and thin, and a special thanks to Tami, who makes me believe everything is possible and good.

PREFACE

Poetry is nearer to vital truth than history.

—Plato, *Ion*

R.E.M. is part lies, part heart, part truth and part garbage.

—Peter Buck

Tell all the Truth but tell it slant—
Success in Circuit lies
Too bright for our infirm Delight
The Truth's superb surprise

As Lightning to the Children eased
With explanation kind
The Truth must dazzle gradually
Or every man be blind—

—Emily Dickinson

Don't dissect us in a clinical, linear way;
come at it from somewhere else.

—Michael Stipe

Poetry is nobody's business except the poet's,
and everybody else can fuck off.

—Philip Larkin

This is a book about a record. But it's also a book about a life that adopted that record as a kind of soundtrack. By which this life discovered some of its narrative, its trajectory, its set pieces and blocking, its phraseology and drama, on a stage that made sense when sense itself was theater. This book is to that record as film is to the stage, as memory is to sound.

The story doesn't get any tidier, unfortunately, because this book is also kind of a soundtrack in and of itself, a soundtrack to a pretend film about the life that produced the book. This is a play that begins when the curtains close and the orchestra retires, and instead of coming up, the lights fade out.

To begin with, one thing this book definitely is *not* is a straightforward biography of the band. There are already plenty of those out there to choose from, comprehensive works which I couldn't improve on or add anything to if I tried.[1] But that's an entirely different imperative anyway, because this book is less contingent on the lives of the members of the band than it is on the life of its author, and that's a fatal premise for a biography.

But isn't that how we feel about records we love—that without us, they wouldn't exist? That they continue to mediate your existence, even after you shut off the stereo, shelve the record, "outgrow" the band? Fandom of this kind knows that if a tree fell in a forest with no one around to hear it, not only would it not make a sound, it wouldn't have been there in the first place. A soundtrack inextricable from the life living it. We thought the forest into existence. As Francisco Varela once wrote, "Every act of knowing brings forth a world." I made *Murmur* as much as it made me.

Such that it's hard to tell what's been made, subject from object, the maker from the predicate, the beholder from the beholden. When I started writing this book, I worried that I wouldn't be able to hear this album with selfish fourteen-year-old ears again—or worse, that I'd have no choice but to. Then I stopped worrying, since both are impossible.

Varela, a philosopher of science as well as a Buddhist, called it *structural drift*—the notion that living organisms change over the course of their lifespan to the degree that they are never the same organism they were even a short while earlier. The cells are different, the skeleton regenerates itself every ten years, the ear cells and the brain cell colonies that heard a song for the first time no longer exist, just a shaky continuity floating along a chain of moments. We jeopardize our grasp on something as concrete as a rock album—a *record*, i.e., a document to defeat time—through our own ongoing self-production. We can also call it *autopoeisis*, as Varela did: that growing rift between us and fourteen-year-old ears.

That teenager is gone, but his thoughts still drift around. His ears are here too, but now they're mine. His feelings have become my notions, his battered copy of *Murmur* shines dull and black on my turntable. Whose favorite album is being written about here? We can't even agree on our favorite songs, a jury of two hung by anything but lack of evidence. The jury is excused. The life that once needed the soundtrack has gone to the same place as the ears that delivered the one to the other and the air that first animated them all in sound.

*   *   *

In researching the reference to Laocoön, the Hellenic figure Michael Stipe mentions in the song "Laughing," I happened across Richard Brilliant's *My Laocoön*. His book is essentially about how a personal experience of a work of art can become tainted by what history has to say about it. Brilliant argues that history divorced the famous statue of Laocoön in the Vatican Museum—known to antiquarians by the shorthand of *The Laocoön*—from the mythological event it's supposed to portray:

> The babble of tongues—Greek, Latin, German, Italian, and even English—seeming to emanate from the Laocoön and its abundant historiographic and critical texts not only compounds the difficulty of deciphering the statue for whatever it is, or was, but also brings to the fore the necessity of understanding my predecessors' understanding of the work prior to attempting to understand the sculpture myself.

He continues:

> To my great consternation, I found that among art historians who constantly engage in the interpretation of artworks, there seemed to be little appreciation either of the complexity of the interpretive act or of the ability of earlier interpretations to restrain the imagination of subsequent generations, even when the conceptual or factual basis of those interpretations no longer obtained.

The strategy that Brilliant develops is to triangulate several different versions of the Laocoön statue in order to arrive at a dehistoricized understanding of both the work and the myth, which he calls *My Laocoön*. Brilliant's effort to reconcile public history with personal experience mirrored my process in trying to capture *Murmur*.

Although this is a *record*—i.e., a document to defeat time—it's not made of stone. It's not a statue in a park that you can walk around and touch and register its shifting shadows on your skin. If it's problematic to think about a "solid thing of marble, existing in real space" as a "text to be read," as Brilliant points out in *My Laocoön*, *Murmur* presents an even greater conundrum. *Murmur* is part object (the sleeve, the vinyl), part text (the lyrics, which are indeterminate), and part performance—a thing, but also a document of that thing. Unlike Michelangelo, who saw a finished sculpture in a block of marble and only claimed to "free it," in the course of writing this book I felt I was trying to free *My Murmur* from a block of marble that is already *The Murmur*, not knowing how different those two things are or how similar. Just where do the boundaries of *Murmur* lie, or for that matter, *anything* that seems to be more that it is? How do you find its surfaces, much less read what's written on them? *Murmur* is indisputably mythological, like the Laocoön. How meaningful is it to fix that mythology in the marble of the written word?

Questions like these lead to a host of potential problems. One is that this book is implicitly supposed to *explain* something, which is very nearly the opposite of what *Murmur*'s worth is to me. *Murmur* was, and is, about not understanding things too quickly or too assuredly. An artist wants his or her work to be "understood," but by a particular means also inscribed as a part of that work. Therefore, it would be as equally disheartening to me for one of the band to read this and feel I had succeeded in explaining away the record's mystery as it would if he felt I utterly misunderstood it and glossed the whole damn thing.

Another problem is that every *idea* along the way has also been written about in its own book, each twice the size of this one and at least that many times more competently explained. I can only try to document how some of these ideas first found purchase in my head through the sounds on *Murmur* before I had an inkling that these ideas were even anything like ideas. And as we emerge from the feeling that records are all about us, we move into another common feeling, which is to want to know why they're not.

So here's how it's going to go down. The first chapter begins with a quick thumbnail sketch of the early history of the band leading up to the recording of *Murmur*, and then what follows is a portrait of the studio environment and how it was important in the making of the album. This sets the stage for chapter two, where I move through the album track-by-track and note-by-note. You'll probably need a break after this much detail, so I shift gears for the second half of the book. Chapter three begins with my initial experience of the record and a dose of historical context, and then I step through the looking glass, so to speak, for an analysis of the album cover. This leads into a discussion of Gothic, which eventually begins to fold in some of the musical detail from the first half of the book. Then I step back out of the looking glass onto Georgia soil again with some observations about 80s culture, Southern Gothic, and my experiences living in the South. In the fourth and final chapter, a lot of the stuff I've covered up to that point is brought to bear in my analysis of *Murmur*'s vocals and language. The appendix contains my interpretations of the album's lyrics, and is the source from which I'll be quoting throughout the book.

One thing you may notice as you read through the book is that the writing style morphs a bit from section to section or even from passage-to-passage. Don't let it throw you—this is a complex record, and I think a variety of approaches are warranted in sussing out its various aspects. Some parts are densely technical, others are more prose-like; some are more journalistic, others like diary entries. This is my personal soundtrack, my mix tape, but I welcome you to fast-forward through any parts you may find difficult or less interesting and move on to the other sections.

I want to conclude here by saying that this book is not entirely meant to bridge art and audience, but to exist as something parallel to both art and audience, which is the netherland from which I first heard *Murmur*. I hoped to render it as such, and I hope you'll enjoy it as such. Above all, I hope you'll discover a few things about *Murmur* that you might not have thought about before, as I definitely did while writing this book. This goes for you too, R.E.M., because your right to spectatorship of your own art is at least as sacred as anyone else's. This netherland is claimed on your behalf.

J. Niimi
Chicago, Thanksgiving 2004
jniimi@uchicago.edu

NOTES

1. For a more detailed account of the band's early days and the band members' personal histories, I recommend the following excellent biographies: *It Crawled from the South: An R.E.M. Companion* by Marcus Gray, *Adventures in Hi-Fi: The Complete R.E.M.* by Rob Jovanovic and Tim Abbott, and *R.E.M. Fiction: An Alternative Biography* by David Buckley. There's also *R.E.M.: From Chronic Town to Monster* by Dave Bowler and Bryan Dray and Denise Sullivan's *Talk About the Passion: An Oral History*, which are both worth checking out. For an interesting if slightly discombobulated first-person history of the early Athens scene, see Rodger Lyle Brown's book *Party Out of Bounds: The B-52's, R.E.M., and the Kids Who Rocked Athens, Georgia*. And for a detailed, if wildly conjectural, interpretation of R.E.M.'s early lyrics, see John A. Platt's book *Murmur* in the now-defunct Classic Rock Albums series.

I.

The four members of R.E.M. loaded their guitars and drums into a decrepit van in mid-January of 1983 and left their home of Athens, Georgia, heading north on I-85. The 200-mile drive took them to Charlotte, North Carolina, where they would begin work on their as-yet-untitled full-length debut album. Vocalist Michael Stipe would later give it the title of *Murmur*, picking it from a list he read somewhere of the seven easiest words to say in the English language.

It was a drive they'd made many times already. Aside from numerous road trips there for club shows—their reputation as a great live act was already spreading throughout the Southern Atlantic states with an un-checked momentum—they'd also recorded a seven-inch single and an EP with North Carolina native Mitch Easter at his Drive-In Studio in Winston-Salem, so named be-cause it was located in his parents' converted garage space. Easter had recorded the band's "Radio Free Europe" single there in April 1981, and the *Chronic Town* EP six months after that. The band had also met their manager

Jefferson Holt after a July 1980 gig in nearby Carrboro where Holt was working the door—R.E.M. was filling in for Pylon, who couldn't make the show. At the time, Holt was managing a record store and was starting to book local shows for out-of-town bands, with a particular interest in the burgeoning Athens scene. It was through Holt that the band decided to work with Easter at Drive-In, after Holt had asked his friend Peter Holsapple for some suggestions about cheap recording studios. The R.E.M. guys were already big fans of Holsapple's band, the dB's, which helped clinch the decision.

Easter's home studio was primitive, but its relaxed atmosphere (guitarist Peter Buck tells stories of Easter's mom bringing the band coffee and donuts), coupled with Easter's complementary pop sensibilities, made it an ideal place for R.E.M. to begin addressing the problem every nascent band encounters: how to translate their road-hewn material to vinyl. This wasn't much of a concern for the band when they recorded their first single with Easter—the "Radio Free Europe"/"Sitting Still" seven-inch, released in a tiny initial pressing of about a thousand copies by their friend Johnny Hibbert on his new "label," Hib-Tone Records. It wasn't even so much of a concern after the band signed to I.R.S. Records and released *Chronic Town*—the label was fine with the idea of starting the band off with an EP release that would break listeners' ears in, while giving the band time to further hone their songs and develop their studio sound. But with the surprise buzz created by "Radio Free Europe" (voted #1 single in the *Village Voice*), as well as the rising cult popularity of the *Chronic Town* EP (especially in England), I.R.S. was now expecting R.E.M. to come up with an album that could capitalize on that underground buzz and parlay it into national recognition. At the same time, the band did not want to make a record that pandered to any of the prevailing radio chart trends: Euro-synth pop, hair metal, and light-rock balladry. More important-ly, they simply couldn't even if they had to. *Murmur* was a giant gamble in a sense, but it was their only choice, and as far as the band were concerned, they had little to lose.

Peter Buck was born in California and moved to Ros-well, Georgia in 1971 at the age of fourteen. He attended Emory University in the Atlanta suburb of Decatur from 1975 to 1977, eventually dropping out to take a job at Wuxtry Records in Athens the following year (where he continued to work off and on until about 1986), teaching himself guitar in his spare time by playing along with records.

It was while working at Wuxtry that Buck struck up a friendship with Michael Stipe. Stipe was born in Decatur, Georgia, but moved around in his childhood due to his father's army career, living briefly in Germany and at-tending high school in Southern Illinois, near East St. Louis. Stipe moved to Athens in the late 1970s to study art at the University of Georgia, and met Buck in early 1979. Stipe and his two sisters were regulars at Wuxtry, and he would come in to browse the racks and talk about bands with Buck, who often noodled around on his guitar while manning the counter. Eventually the conversation came around to starting a band themselves.

Buck was living in a deconsecrated church on Oconee Street in Athens, the former St. Mary's Episcopal Church, which was sublet by Dan Wall, Buck's employer at Wuxtry. The dilapidated church was subdivided into crude bedrooms, with a large space in the back perfectly suited for band practices (as well as some of the college town's notoriously raucous parties). Buck's roommate and sometime girlfriend Kathleen O'Brien introduced him to her friend Bill Berry, whom she had met in the UGA dorms. Berry was born in Minnesota and moved to Macon, Georgia with his family in 1972 as a young teen.

It was back in Macon that Berry first encountered Mike Mills, a fellow high school student. Mills is arguably the band's closest thing to a "native" Southerner: though he too was born in California, like Buck, Mills's parents moved to Georgia while he was still a baby. As a teenager Mills was a clean-cut straight-A student, while the teenage Berry was something of a long-haired stoner, and the pair did not get along well until the day they both happened to show up at the same band audition and reluctantly decided to bury the hatchet (as Berry had already set up his drum kit and thus couldn't bail out of the rehearsal). The two ended up becoming best friends, playing together in a few different bands (including one called the Frustrations, which included a local guitarist by the name of Ian Copeland). The duo eventually moved to Athens together in 1979 to enroll at UGA.

The four future members of R.E.M. were finally introduced to one another by Kathleen O'Brien in the fall of 1979. It was a less than auspicious beginning: Stipe was put off by Mills's falling-down drunkenness, but he did like Berry's now-famous monobrow, which Stipe credits for tipping the scale in his decision to join up with the two Maconites. A few months later, O'Brien was planning a party at the church on Oconee Street in celebration of her birthday, to be held on April 5, 1980. She had gotten the popular local band the Side Effects to agree to play, but she now needed an "opening act." She asked the as-yet-unnamed (in fact, barely formed) R.E.M. to play as well. The band was thrilled at the prospect and said yes, though they had only a couple of half-hearted, beer-soaked rehearsals under their belt by this point.

Buck and Stipe had written a few tentative songs together before they met Berry and Mills. Together the four of them worked out a few more originals, as well as a slew of covers, rehearsing in the back of the church during the Winter of 1979–80. After O'Brien's invitation to play came in February, the band kicked up the pace, cobbling together a set's worth of songs in the weeks before the party, deciding at the last minute on the name Twisted Kites (after discarding such other possibilities as Negro Eyes and Cans of Piss—though some band members claim that they played the party without any name at all).

About three hundred people showed up at the church that night, surpassing even O'Brien's expectations: the birthday gathering was now an Event. After the Side Effects finished their set, Twisted Kites/R.E.M./untitled took the stage, playing about twenty songs, roughly half of them originals, to a wildly enthusiastic (and profoundly drunk) crowd. The band was so well received that night, in fact, that the crowd goaded them into playing their entire set a second time. Among the covers reportedly included in the set were "Honky Tonk Women," "God Save the Queen," "Secret Agent Man," the Troggs' "I Can't Control Myself," and the Monkees' "(I'm Not Your) Steppin' Stone." Among the band's originals that night (also documented on the early bootleg *Bodycount at Tyrone's*, recorded about six months after the party—a fairly representative cross-section of the band's early material[1]) was a nascent version of "Just a Touch," which appeared in final form on *Lifes Rich Pageant* in 1986.

Their earliest material was fast, brash, and goofy. Most of the lyrics were first person narratives from Stipe directed, interestingly enough, toward women subjects (or possibly *against* women subjects, as some R.E.M. historians believe). There's a liberal use of the rock pronoun *baby*, and plenty of *I don't wanna*s a la the first Ramones record. The band settled on the name R.E.M., picked from a dictionary—it didn't have any trite "punk" connotations, and Stipe really liked the periods. Plus, like *Murmur*, it was easy to pronounce.

The band was an almost instant hit on the Athens scene. But as they started to venture out of town, they realized that maybe they weren't just a local beer-party phenomenon. With encouragement from Jefferson Holt—who had moved to Athens to manage the band—they decided to try and record a demo to send out to clubs and record labels. The band's first "recording session" was held on June 6, 1980, a couple months after their gig at the church party, in the back of the Decatur branch of Wuxtry Records, where Buck had worked as a student at Emory. It was a stop-off on the afternoon of their first out of town gig at the Warehouse in neighboring Atlanta, essentially a rehearsal for the show, and they bashed through eight songs while Wuxtry owner Mark Methe videotaped them. (While the band never used the tape, which sounded like crap, the murky audio track of the session has shown up on various bootlegs over the years as *first demos*.)

Holt suggested they make a proper recording to showcase their newer songs, so they booked a day at engineer Joe Perry's Bombay Studio, a small eight-track setup in nearby Smyrna, in February of 1981. Within a matter of hours the band laid down eight songs, including skeletal versions of "Radio Free Europe," "Sitting Still," and "Shaking Through." Though the tapes have never been made public, the results were apparently less than stellar— Holt urged the band not to send them around and went looking for another studio and engineer. At the suggestion of Peter Holsapple, Holt called Mitch Easter.

Easter recorded the band's seven-inch on April 15, 1981, in his garage studio setup. The band wisely decided to focus on just a few songs, rather than banging out a whole mini-set as they did at Bombay, so they recorded "Radio Free Europe" and "Sitting Still," as well as a third song, "White Tornado"—a quasi-surf instrumental they had just written. The band slapped together a few hundred handmade cassettes of the three songs (plus a "dub mix" of "Radio Free Europe" that Easter had later spliced together, half-jokingly) and sent the tape out to clubs, labels, magazines, and just about anyplace else they could think of. Hib-Tone released the seven-inch of "Radio Free Europe" b/w "Sitting Still" in July 1981; of the initial pressing of 1,000 copies, 600 were sent out as promos, and a total of around 6,000 additional copies were later pressed by popular demand (amazingly, since the first pressing mistakenly omitted any contact info for the label). The band was annoyed with the muddy-sounding mastering job (Buck smashed one of his copies and nailed it to a wall in his house), but the single spurred a critical buzz for the band, garnering wide-spread plaudits and landing on a number of year-end Top 10 lists. R.E.M. started to get letters from labels, most of which made them laugh. They threw them in the fireplace and kept playing.

*   *   *

The band played a high-profile show in Atlanta that previous winter—their biggest yet—opening for the Police at the Fox Theater in December 1980. They landed the prestigious gig through Bill Berry's old friend from Macon, Ian Copeland (brother of Police drummer Stewart Copeland), to whom Berry had been sending the band's rehearsal and demo tapes. Ian was now running F.B.I., a successful booking agency that handled the Police, among other I.R.S. acts, and had been bugging his brother, Miles Copeland, the president of I.R.S., to sign R.E.M. Miles had heard the band's cruddy demo cassette and wasn't that impressed, but he eventually capitulated in the face of Ian's hyperbolic praise, dispatching I.R.S. VP Jay Boberg to New Orleans in March of 1982 to check out the band in person. The show that night was at a drug-infested dive called The Beat Exchange, where the toilets in the bathrooms were clogged with used syringes. The night was by all accounts a disaster—the Rastafarian sound man wandered off before their set started, and the band, uncharacteristically, suffered from horrible stage fright. But Boberg was sold, and upon returning to LA he advised Miles Copeland to sign R.E.M. The band adjourned to the label's New York office in May 1982 to sign a five-record deal. I.R.S. bought the master tapes the band had recorded with Easter and released *Chronic Town* in August 1982, with plans for a full-length album release the following spring.

*   *   *

Reflection Sound Studios in Charlotte looks pretty much like any recording studio that dates to the early 70s, when audio electronics began to enter the consumer market—a market that included both the people who consumed music and the people who wanted to make it themselves. Only five years earlier, recording studios were still building their own equipment with solder and sheet metal. Beyond companies with the wherewithal to employ engineers (real engineers, with professional training in electrical and mechanical engineering), having a viable recording setup not backed by radio revenues was the domain of amateur hobbyists, some of whom served in military capacities (like the army signal corps, where unlimited access to cutting-edge technology first whetted these hobbyists' appetites for audio experimentation).

With advancements in the electronic manufacturing industries (centered around the refinement of the transistor), these folks could now buy high-quality, reasonably priced mass-produced gear in place of their primitive homebrew inventions or costly, hard-to-come-by European products designed for broadcast applications and state-funded budgets. Now they were able to get down to what they wanted to do in the first place beyond all the soldering irons and the oscilloscopes, which was to make music. In turn some of these people built commercial recording studios to subsidize their dual interest in what was essentially folk technology and folk art. Though it's easy to take both for granted today, without independent studios there would be no independent music.

Not being affiliated with any particular record label or company, Reflection Sound Studios serviced a wide range of musical genres and clientele. It was outfitted with a modest array of professional grade recording equipment and musical gear, and could be rented by the hour or by the day by anyone, with or without the services of one of its house engineers. Reflection's layout was typical of many studios at the time, a plan that's still commonly used today in the construction of studios: A central control room contains all the recording equipment, adjacent to a larger studio room where the band plays, with a sound-proofed double-pane glass window connecting the two and providing a sightline between the engineer and the band. The control room at Reflection is elevated slightly above the level of the live room, looking down into it, and is accessible by a small staircase in the hallway outside the live room.[2]

Inside the live studio room, connected by another door and window, is a smaller, closet-like "isolation booth," an enclosed, acoustically treated space where loud things like amps or a drum kit can be placed so as not to interfere with the other instruments. Like a lot of studios, Reflection also has a smaller second studio room, although R.E.M. did not utilize it on *Murmur*—in fact, there were other sessions in progress there during the recording of the album. The band even dropped in on one Studio B session during a lull in *Murmur* to contribute handclaps to another band's record. As far as the studio was concerned, R.E.M. was just one anonymous group out of many that were booked at Reflection over the course of January and February 1983—probably less notable by virtue of being a rock band.

Running an independent recording studio in any city is a treacherous business, but especially so in a small city off the mainstream record industry's map—Charlotte is a good seven-hour drive from Nashville and ten hours from New York City. Luckily, Reflection's setup was ideally suited to its bread-and-butter clientele—Southern gospel and soul groups. Reflection's main live room, Studio A, is an open thirty- by forty-five-foot wood paneled space designed in such a way that not only can it accommodate a modern gospel choir and band (plus its drummer in the isobooth), the room's acoustical properties are uniquely suited to the genre as well. The room is "live," or acoustically reflective, enough for voices to sound natural singing in it, but controlled enough to allow engineers to capture their sound with relative ease, without the technical problems that often arise when there are a lot of microphones capturing a lot of people producing a lot of sound in one enclosed space. As *Murmur* engineer Don Dixon put it in recording slang, "[Reflection's Studio A] was just the right combination of live and dead." The main room's sonic properties probably lent themselves to the duality of the studio's name: a space designed with a sensitivity for acoustical reflection, as well as the more spiritual kind—much like a church or a cathedral. In 2003, two Grammy Award-nominated gospel albums were made at Reflection.

While anyone would be hard-pressed to describe R.E.M. as a gospel act, it's interesting to think about how the studio's legacy might have resonated with the band during their stay at Reflection. They were still in the Bible Belt, but they were now in a different house of devotion, where soul musicians came to make Christian records (and vice versa)[3], a place that also happened to be sanctioned by musically like-minded hipsters like Dixon and Easter. It's reasonable to imagine that the band must have thought about their own devotion and austerity in such a place, both in terms of the band's sound and the personal life that each was starting to give up in the name of music.

Murmur was a new kind of sacrifice for a band that was becoming accustomed to sacrifice—after all, being in a band, as anyone who's ever been in one can attest, is not so much about freedom as it is about the giving up of one kind of burden for another. If the open road and the creative lifestyle do afford an escape of sorts, going into the studio is an equally profound time of confrontation, a kind of reckoning. The most intense recording sessions are fueled by an energy that's a lot like religion—a concentrated time when individual needs and egos are put aside in the attempt to galvanize a higher collective mind, especially when the stakes are high, as they were for R.E.M. by 1983. By comparison, the making of *Chronic Town* was a sleepover. Here the four of them lived together like monks in the squalor of a cheap hotel room for three weeks; rock stars don't steal ketchup packets from Burger King just to have something to eat with the stale tortillas they scavenge from the back of the van. But what they ate and how they slept only defined their existence—their lives during those weeks were defined at Reflection. There was penance and ecstasy and catharsis. It sucked, but how much more could it suck otherwise? Which is probably an even better description of what church is for.

It ought to be remembered that R.E.M. wrote most of their early songs in the pew of a dilapidated church, where skylight angled down on them through holes in the collapsed ceiling. Birds alighted from their amps when they came to practice. Peter Buck even used the phrase "spooky gospel" to describe the sound of *Chronic Town*'s "Gardening at Night." Buck lived in a church, but Stipe would have been comfortable there too—he was christened John Michael Stipe, after John Wesley—a choice informed by his Methodist grandfather who was a preacher in Georgia. A year after the *Murmur* sessions, during the recording of *Reckoning*, Stipe jokingly grabbed a gospel album out of a closet at Reflection and sang its liner notes over the backing track of "Seven Chinese Brothers" as a warm-up exercise. Beyond the parts where Stipe cracks up and his cadence falls off, it's startling how effortlessly Stipe could make lines like "the joy of knowing Jesus" fit the music, as if his vocal delivery had always been an arcane kind of preaching masked only by his usually obtuse lyrics.[4] In fact, there's an underlying sense of the grandson-of-a-preacher-man throughout *Murmur*'s imagery and language. In "Pilgrimage," Stipe sings, "speaking in tongues / it's worth a broken lip," bringing Pentecostal notions of authenticity to bear on his own cryptic lyrical style. "Talk About the Passion" has the quasi-Christian refrain "not everyone can carry the weight of the world." And the existential turmoil in "Perfect Circle" is resolved in its chorus of "heaven assumed"—a notion later revisited, in Classical terms, in the idea of "dreams of Elysian" from "West of the Fields."

But Reflection was also a good choice because it was geographically convenient for everyone involved. The band was already comfortable making the trek from Athens. They set up shop at the nearby Coliseum Motel on Independence Boulevard, sleeping two to a cot. They didn't enjoy the comfort of sympathetic fans and their beds this time around, but they also didn't suffer from the distraction, or the fatigue of vertical sleep in a smelly van. Mitch Easter and Don Dixon lived about an hour's drive away in the Winston-Salem area, and made the daily commute. On most days they worked from noon to midnight, going their separate ways at the end of the day (except for one detour to a local moviehouse to see the movie *Strange Invaders*, in which their song "1,000,000" makes a brief appearance).

Charlotte was cheap then as it still is today. If the band had opted to make the album in New York or LA, most of their tiny budget probably would have been blown in the first week—nowadays, R.E.M. probably spends *Murmur*'s budget on a typical album's catering bills. And this was one tight budget indeed. Easter and Dixon reportedly split a $3,000 advance between the two of them in order to make the record, with the total budget for the record topping out at a paltry $15,000. As Dixon told me:

> We were on a very strict budget—both Mitch and I took substantial pay cuts to do the record—but we believed in the band, and believed that the studio was

a good value. It was handy to all of our home bases, it was out of the mainstream music cities—so the label couldn't pop in whenever they wanted—and it allowed for a certain *je ne sais quoi* that appealed to the band.

And beyond money and geography, Reflection was the obvious choice for more artistic reasons. Although the band wanted to continue working with Easter as producer, they both knew it was time to move up from the garage to a more versatile and more hi-fi environment. Although Easter was well versed in studio practice and was sympathetic to R.E.M.'s ideas, he wasn't totally comfortable bringing the band into a new studio as the primary engineer. Easter knew and trusted Dixon, who already had experience at Reflection as an engineer and as a recording artist.

Reflection had a number of technical advantages over Mitch's home studio, where *Chronic Town* and the "Radio Free Europe" single were recorded. Unlike a lot of independent studios, Reflection had an inside connection with the sales reps at MCI, the manufacturers of top-end studio equipment—a relationship that not only ensured privileged access to state-of-the-art products, but also the specialized servicing necessary for the constant maintenance of complex and sometimes temperamental pro audio gear. In terms of nuts-and-bolts, Reflection's Studio A boasted a 36-input MCI 600 mixing console ("The snazzy one with the plasma display," as Easter recounts)—an industry workhorse that, beyond its clean circuitry and well-designed architecture, also allowed for increased tracking flexibility as compared with Drive-In's smaller Quantum 24-input console. The extra tracks gave the engineers and the band more elbow room in terms of instrumental tracking, sound treatment, and mixing. Reflection also featured a two-inch 24-track MCI tape deck, which offered sharper fidelity over Easter's one-inch 16-track, as well as more room for various engineering techniques, such as retaining multiple takes of Stipe's vocals in order to edit the best parts of each down to one superlative final track.

Still, it would be somewhat simplistic and disingenuous to say that R.E.M. was "limited" by the parameters of Easter's home recording setup on their earlier recordings. The transcendent, organic production on the Easter-produced *Chronic Town* EP not only makes you doubt that the band's vision could ever have been realized had they gone the more conventional route in 1982 (big label/ big studio/big producer . . . and they had numerous offers along these lines), but also that the EP would ever have garnered a fraction of the oddball mystique that ultimately gave the band the agency and leverage to make *Murmur* and make it on their own terms. This was before indie rock (and even "college rock"), so the irony may be lost now that back then the easiest and most direct way to make a record was to *get* a major label contract, not to be so quixotic and dumb as to try and make one yourself. Yet this is exactly what Easter and the band had succeeded in doing, against most odds.

Chronic Town succeeded as a fully realized expression of R.E.M.'s aesthetic because Easter was one of the craftiest engineers in the 80s in terms of being able to thrive within technical (and budgetary) limitations—not to mention the fact that Easter was working with an exceptional band with exceptional song material. Still, Easter's studio space was only barely conducive to recording ("a twenty-four-by twenty-four-foot ex-garage with extremely hard walls and a low ceiling," as he describes), and judging from R.E.M.'s earlier abortive attempts at recording (and in well-appointed places like New York's RCA Studios), Easter's resourcefulness and attentive ears were the main things that made up for what were otherwise extremely modest circumstances. Reflection's equipment, on the other hand, allowed Easter and the band to exercise a similar creative freedom in the studio but with fewer logistical worries. The increased fidelity was only a plus—not to mention the fact that Easter was freed up by Dixon's presence behind the console, now able to focus more of his energies on things like arranging and production, as well as being able to jump in front of a mic when he felt like it to lay down an overdub or two on guitar or the vibes.

In terms of its other tech knickknacks, Reflection's modest arsenal showed discreet taste, even by 2005 standards. The studio boasted an excellent collection of high-quality vintage microphones (like the vacuum-tube Neumann U47, whose globe-like foam windscreen reminded Stipe of Angela Davis), as well as choice signal processing gear like compressors (a couple of UREI 1176s, which are an engineer's '65 Mustang), exotic new digital delays (like the Lexicon Model 200, at the time the Lamborghini Countach of digital reverbs), and a few cherry perks, such as the studio's tube EMT plate reverb.[5] As Easter said, "Reflection was essentially comparable to any studio anywhere, gear-wise." As such, Dixon and Easter didn't find it necessary to bring any of their own gear, except for a few signature musical instruments. Easter brought along his white Fender Electric XII twelve-string guitar (a gift from his father when he turned thirteen; Peter Buck did not own an electric Rickenbacker twelve-string at this point, contrary to fan myth), as well as his trusty Danelectro electric sitar (which Buck had used in the *Chronic Town* session, most prominently on "Gardening at Night"). Easter's Electric XII can also be heard on many of Let's Active's early recordings.

Peter Buck's workhorse amp—his Fender Twin—was broken at the time, so Easter loaned him his checkerboard-grill Ampeg Gemini II for the session, which was used on most tracks, alongside the studio's little solid state (i.e., transistor rather than tube-driven) Kasino amp. Guitar-wise, Buck had brought his maple-glo Rickenbacker 360, which he had also used on the *Chronic Town* session. Mike Mills had been using a Dan Armstrong bass up to the time of *Chronic Town*, but Easter lent him his Rickenbacker 4001 bass on an early garage session, and by the time of the *Murmur* sessions Mills had bought his own. Mills played through the studio's trusty Ampeg B-15, which was set up in the hallway outside the live room. Dixon recalls Bill Berry using the studio's Sonor drum kit, set up in Studio A's isolation booth, which everyone called the "Tiki Hut" for its cedar-shingled conical ceiling. Easter remembers wanting to set Bill up in the main room, but Berry, in his ratty Steel Pulse T-shirt, liked the weird little space and was excited to play drums in there—it was how he envisioned a studio session was supposed to be.

Easter, Dixon, and the band availed themselves of the studio's two pianos (a modern Yamaha and an old upright "tack" piano—so called because of the thumbtacks inserted on its hammers to compensate for the dark sound of its enclosed harp), its Hammond B-3 organ, its Wurlitzer, and the somewhat unusual presence of a vintage Musser vibraphone. These instruments played a big part in *Murmur*'s sound, and in resolving the band's aesthetic concerns. Dixon explains:

> I wanted to create a Stax-like sound in the balance of the overall mix. Vocals as part of a drum-driven groove. A big reason for this was the desire on the part of the band for the guitars to be very clean. Guitars were kind of "out" at the time, and fuzz guitars were scary to the band and the label. The best model I could think of to keep a heavy groove was the sound of old Stax records. With [these organic-sounding instruments] as part of the studio's standing arsenal, we had the tools we needed to accomplish that.

As is common studio practice, the band recorded the basic tracks for most songs playing together live—drums, bass, and guitars, and probably a "guide vocal" from Stipe—with the instruments acoustically isolated from one another. Buck's guitar amp was set up in the main room, Berry's drum kit was in the isolation booth, Mills's bass amp was in the outside hallway, and Stipe was in the space under the stairwell behind the control room (he didn't want anyone to see him sing). The band monitored themselves over headphones. Often in recording sessions, a band might start by recording the basic tracks for all the songs on the album, then go back and overdub the rest of the instruments and the vocals. However, for the *Murmur* sessions, the band proceeded one song at a time, recording all of its tracks—the live tracks as well as the overdubs—before moving on to the next song. For the most part, the band would record the basic tracks together, then one person at a time would work with Dixon and Easter on overdubs, while the rest of the band played pool in the other room or went to get something to eat. Generally the band was able to nail most songs within a few takes, having played most of the album's material exhaustively over the preceding months on the road.

The majority of *Murmur*'s live tracks were recorded using standard "close miking" technique, where a microphone is placed directly in front of an instrument in order to capture a clean and up-front sound. But in terms of overdubs, Easter and Dixon sometimes took advantage of Studio A's natural acoustics by employing "room miking," or placing a microphone at a distance from an instrument. This technique can be used to create a sense of space in a recording, or to create unusual effects. Reflection had a number of sound processing devices that could electronically recreate the sound of a room—or a gymnasium or a dungeon, for that matter—but Dixon and Easter's use of room miking was in line with the band's insistence on clean, natural sounds and acoustic, organic-sounding instruments. Devices such as digital reverbs and delay units offer the engineer many options as far as "juicing up" the sound of a recorded track, but often they can sound artificial and obtrusive. On *Murmur* Easter and Dixon strike a harmonious balance between electronic effects and natural ones.

Going into the *Murmur* sessions, the band already had a finished version of "Pilgrimage" in the can, recorded a few weeks earlier by Easter and Dixon as a "test" song over the course of a day or two at Reflection. Though the band was adamant about working with Easter and Dixon, I.R.S. had wanted proof that the two were right for the job. Reportedly, the label wasn't that excited at how "Pilgrimage" turned out, but the band stonewalled them anyway, booking time at Reflection in January 1983 to begin work on the album with Easter and Dixon. The crew worked on the album on and off for about a month over the course of January and February. Since the studio's log book from this period is missing, accounts of the actual amount of time spent in the studio vary: Buck has said it was as low as "about fourteen days," while other estimates have it at around sixteen or seventeen days total, and one accounting puts it as high as twenty-four days.

By all accounts, the album sessions went smoothly—the band played great; Dixon, Easter, and the band got along well (beyond a few heated disagreements about arrangement and production details), and despite a generous amount of beer-quaffing the band was all about business. They disagreed about certain minor decisions, but the band's democratic philosophy prevailed: one of their "rules" was that each member had full veto power about any decision, no matter how minor. Easter describes the atmosphere of the *Murmur* sessions, both within the band, and between the band and Dixon/Easter:

> Jeez, it was pretty civilized. Michael may have sort of been a little removed as the most high-falutin' Artiste in the sense that he had a sort of big-picture view of the sound and was not remotely interested in some

"awesome" sound if he thought it was overbearing. Probably all the rest of the band (and I) might've been a little more teenage/rock 'n' roll in our sensibilities. They'd get a little grumpy, like during the "Perfect Circle" first-listen, but no big deal.

Overall, they were as respectful of each other as any band I can think of, which was remarkable since they really were sort of different "types." They seemed to always grasp the importance of their identity as a unit, and protecting that was important, and that's probably part of why they could seem stodgy at times. They didn't want the outside world to mess them up! Within the band, those guys would mildly insult each other, etc. but it was never mean-spirited . . . In general, they all seemed seriously dedicated to the effort.

Dixon was similarly impressed with the band's sense of identity, as well as the tempered confidence they displayed about their strengths and limitations as a band:

Again, this was an era when you had to be able to play to record. These guys could all play. Would they collectively have made a great Steely Dan cover band? No. Were they creative and musical? Yes. Did they have one of the most unique (and therefore controversial) sounds around? Yes. Were they misunderstood by many fellow musicians, the kinds of guys who would go to the music store and play Joe Satriani licks to show off? Yes.

NOTES

1. It's almost comical to listen to the *Murmur* songs on the band's early bootlegs. The songs were all there,

but the playing is so spastic it's almost hard to believe these guys had aspirations beyond punk. Live, they tried to perform record-collector kitsch as "new wave," and in the confines of the Oconee Street church it made sense, but on these early boots they sound lost— simply *geeks* as opposed to *record* geeks, let alone rock stars or even rockers. But the band was developing confidence in their songwriting sensibilities much faster than confidence in their performative abilities. After *Murmur*, they could now hear their songs in a way that finally let them perform these songs to satisfaction—you can hear the difference on post-1983 bootlegs—and this eventually fed back into their song-writing, enriching it, and they began to have a clearer idea of how to play the songs they wrote, and vice versa.

2. Reflection Sound is still in business: you can view pictures of its facilities at www.reflectionsound.com.

3. The album *Carolina Soul Survey: The Reflection Sound Story* (Grapevine, 2002) chronicles the history of Southern soul acts that recorded at Reflection in the 1970s.

4. This version of the song was eventually released as "Voice of Harold" on *Dead Letter Office* (I.R.S., 1987).

5. Mic geeks might be interested to know that Easter and Dixon hated Shure SM57s, and instead used its red-headed cousin, the SM7, for instrumental tracking—a dumb analogy would be to say that it's a bit like preferring RC over Coke. For ambient room miking, the crew often forsook the sportier AKG C 414 in favor of the more proletarian Electro-Voice 635A, according to Easter—"a cheap omni dynamic, and one of our favorites."

II.

Radio Free Europe

The album opens with a rerecorded version of "Radio Free Europe," the A-side song off the Hib-Tone single (the new version on *Murmur* was also released by I.R.S. as the album's first single). The *Murmur* version differs from the Hib-Tone version in a number of significant ways. The original was played much faster, and more sloppy and garagey; on the album version, the song's tempo has been pulled back a bit, lending it more gravity than the barnstorming take on the Hib-Tone version, while retaining most of the energy of the original. The *Murmur* version is also, needless to say, considerably more hi-fi, and doesn't suffer from the shoddy mastering job on the original seven-inch.

"Radio Free Europe" is an anthem and it isn't: its sing-along chorus is as cathartic sounding as anything U2 has ever written, but what's being insisted upon is anyone's guess. It's been said that the song is about radio as a tool of cultural hegemony—"Spreading cultural imperialism through pop music," as Buck, who came up with the song's title, put it. But it's also thought to speak to censorship in the US; critics point to a notorious article about Stipe's idol Patti Smith in the *Village Voice* (which Stipe subscribed to) entitled "You Can't Say 'Fuck' in Radio Free America." Yet the song also hints at the idea of radio as revolution—"straight off the boat" as a reference to offshore pirate radio in England—as well as a critique of nationalism, with its seeming double-entendre reference to the plight of boat people ("straight off the boat/where to go?"), an issue that loomed large in the 1980s American public consciousness. The song also contains shades of "Holidays in the Sun" and its imagery of Cold War tourism (RFE's "put that up your wall/that this is a country at all"). Buck had been a fan of the Sex Pistols, and went to see them in Atlanta on their ill-fated 1978 American tour—though he was thrown out after sneaking in without a ticket and missed most of the show.

Stipe's vocal on the Hib-Tone RFE is much more reminiscent of his live performances at the time: growlier, more dynamically wide, and slightly off-key in spots.[1] The lyrics on the Hib-Tone single are a bit different from those on the album, and even harder to make out. On the single, Stipe substitutes verse lines for refrain lines and vice versa—showing just how seat-of-the-pants the song's lyrics in fact were. The choruses are slightly different as well—on the single version, it sounds like Stipe is cupping his hands over the mic during the "calling out . . . " line, while this phrase is treated as a separate, reverbed-out overdub on the album version, distinct from the more upfront " . . . in transit."

The Hib-Tone RFE begins with a synth blurt that's reminiscent of the staticky noise that starts off the *Murmur* version, but on the single, it's more identifiable as an actual instrument of the times—that is, an early-80s electronic keyboard. The twangy static that begins the *Murmur* version is a little more difficult to place: It starts off sounding a bit like a jaw harp, gradually rising in pitch until it sounds like water dripping in a cybernetic cave. Its strangeness is the result of an interesting serendipity. This seven-bar-long intro was created by manipulating some errant system hum that had been inadvertently recorded to tape ("Filed away for some future use," as Easter described). Easter triggered this recorded hum with an electronic noise gate that was wired to use Mills's bass part on the "straight off the boat" refrain to open and shut the gate in time with that bass part's attack. The resulting sound was then manually frequency-swept using an EQ knob on the mixing console. This bit was then spliced onto the beginning of the song. After a saturnine belch of reverb, the live part of the song begins. The intro is a sonic rope-a-dope: your ears squint to make sense of this buzzing little noise, only to be pummeled by Bill Berry's thumping tom-tom figure that kicks off the song.

Berry lays down one of his characteristically solid four-to-the-floor beats, augmented by a chirpy shaker sound in the far right speaker on the downbeat during the verses, mirroring the clock-tick of Berry's hi-hat in the left. Stipe's vocal mix during the verse rides a subtle line between loud but incomprehensible and soft but parseable. Buck plays a standard chuggy rock guitar part with a clean dry sound, sticking to the dampened lower strings of the chord except for a up-stroke chordal *ching* on an acoustic guitar, which marks the end of each four-bar repetition throughout the verse. For the pre-chorus "straight off the boat" refrain, Buck then switches to arpeggios—or picking out the individual notes of a chord—and at the end of every four-bar repetition of this is a solid full-chord down-stroke that cleverly makes the refrain a louder mirror of the verse in terms of structure and execution. The last note of the refrain (where Stipe howls "where to go"), Mills hits a low note on the bass that's doubled by the same note on a piano, creating a resonant *dong*. This doubling of instruments is a trick that Easter and Dixon use throughout the course of the record, and it in fact returns later on in the bridge section: a great one-note ascending piano part that's like a doppelganger of Mills's bass in terms of register and timbre, with a funky attack similar to Mills's slapped E-string. Also featured on the bridge are Easter's glinty, triangle-like vibraphone accents, highly compressed to bring out their dissonant overtones.

On the final, doubled chorus, Berry switches dramatically to the ride cymbal for the first, but then goes back to hi-hat for the second chorus, an odd but effective bit of drum arranging. In between, he does a full-kit drum fill like something off of the generally more live-sounding *Chronic Town*. The song ends with an electric Buck arpeggio borrowed from the refrain, and, in what would be one of the last instances of this in an R.E.M. single, a resolution back to the tonic chord—A major—with a final vibe hit from Mitch ringing out dissonantly behind it.

Pilgrimage

Before RFE's fade-out has a chance to dissolve into silence we start to hear Stipe's "take a turn" vocal begin to fade in—a ghostly effect created by using just the feed from the EMT plate reverb by itself without the source vocal track that it would commonly be mixed back in with. This song was recorded in December 1982 in a separate session from *Murmur* as a sort of demo for I.R.S., though Easter and Dixon encouraged the band to try to make it as much of a finished, releasable song as possible. Their attention to detail paid off, and rather than rerecording it, this initial "tryout" track was ultimately chosen for inclusion on the album.[2] Easter credits this song—one of his favorites—as "establishing the mood of the record." At 4:25, it's the longest song on the album (the rest clock in at a radio-friendly average of around three-and-a-half minutes, except for the four-minute-long RFE).

The fade-in suits the song's fugal structure, where one basic melodic theme is slowly permutated throughout the song's verse sections. After an ambient-sounding vocal/piano intro, the song snaps into the foreground with the appearance of the drums and bass. In this first verse a piano doubles the bass part, much like the bridge section of RFE, the two instruments almost indistinguishable—a subtle touch. After a few rounds, Buck's guitar joins in, doubling the same six-note figure. Easter joins in with the Musser vibes on the second verse, harmonizing the six notes. The drum tracks on the song are relatively untreated, with the only obvious reverb effect showing up on Berry's tom fills as a thunderous accent behind the "escape momentum" lyric. The acoustic guitar here, and throughout *Murmur*, is Easter's 1956 Gibson LG-1, which Buck also used on *Chronic Town*—as Easter says, "a small, bottom-of-the-line model which still has that excellent projecting midrange that is characteristic of Gibsons. This one is sort of bass-light and hard-sounding, which makes it perfect in the rock band setting." The ending chorus features some tasty percussion accents: tambourine, Berry playing bongos in the background, and what sounds like a drumstick on a metal garbage can lid. The song ends with the fluttering motorized vibrato sound from Easter's vibes.

Laughing

This song about "Laocoön and *her* two sons"[3] is an example of extremely skillful production and arranging on the part of Dixon and Easter—it builds to a tangible climax without seeming to get louder or denser in the process. Whatever mechanical "punch-ins" there are in the song (i.e., sectional overdubs) are executed with subtlety and aplomb: when you finally become aware of a sound, it's because it had already been introduced almost subliminally in an earlier part of the song, and only as a variation of a more overt part occurring at the time.

Berry's reggae-inflected rototom intro recalls their labelmates the Police, as well as Easter's one-time description of Berry's early drum parts as "weird ska." The rototoms—high-pitched drums consisting of a small plastic drum head mounted on a steel frame, without a reverberant shell or bottom head like traditional toms—are played in the right channel and reverbed across to the left channel. The intro continues in faux-reggae mode, with a sparse bass drum and hi-hat beat behind Mills's snaky bass line and more syncopated rototom bursts. It's a jarring sound after "Pilgrimage's" languid ending, and an interesting sequencing choice: After this unstable, musically ambiguous-sounding intro, the song could go anywhere—it could burst into a straightforward rocker like "Radio Free Europe," or return to the down-tempo strum of a song like "Pilgrimage." Instead it finds a third level, reminiscent of some of the sounds on the earlier two songs, but with a new kind of mood and feel.

Berry ends the intro with a fill on standard toms and comes in again with one of his trademark four-to-the-floor kick/snare/hi-hat beats. He's joined by the bass, and some pensive acoustic guitar arpeggios played by Buck. The backing vocals are intimate and up-front here, contrasted with Mills's washed-out harmonies on "Pilgrimage." There's a single-note piano line low in the chorus part, which functions almost like a second bass line. These kinds of melodic, single-note piano lines heard throughout *Murmur* give Mills the space to play the more harmonically complex bass figures he's fond of, and they also carry melodic weight during the times when he's playing the simpler, "walking"-type bass lines he's also prone toward.

A strummy acoustic guitar replaces Buck's arpeggios for the "lighted in a room" refrain, continuing into the chorus, when it's joined by a veritable orchestra of strummed acoustic chords. Easter described this section as the "campfire" part: Dixon and Easter picked up guitars and joined Buck in the live room, where they gathered around one mic to lay down three simultaneous unison guitars parts (here Easter availed Dixon of his Gibson B-25-12N, which he had also brought from home). They then tracked *another* "campfire" overdub, after detuning the tape deck's varispeed by a fraction of a hair—an engineering trick that creates a wider sound by making that one track almost imperceptibly out-of-tune with the rest of the song, thus differentiating it in the mix from what would otherwise be a similar-sounding track.

Easter recalls another trick the crew employed to enhance the guitar sound on "Laughing":

> One thing we used a lot on the strummy bits was the "Nashville" tuning, where you borrow the high G from a twelve-string set. This does amazing things, since the G string is often problematic tuning-wise when you go from E-position chords to others. The high string (up one octave) lifts this note away from the rest and the whole thing gets clear and pretty. There's another version which replaces *all* the wound strings with the twelve-string octave ones—I don't think we ever did that, but that makes a lovely zithery sound over a regular guitar.

Swirling arpeggios then make their entrance on the second chorus—Buck's electric guitar run through the motorized Leslie 147 speaker cabinet from the studio's Hammond B-3 organ. Easter adds: "We would have felt like sissies using [an electronic device like] a flange pedal . . . although we would have been pleased with ourselves had we done actual tape flanging" (referring to the tandem-tape-machine technique invented by Les Paul and popularized by the Beatles and Jimi Hendrix, which derived its name from the "playing" of the flange of a tape reel to create the swooshing, out-of-phase effect often heard in pop songs).

Bill's braying background harmony fills out the rest of the chorus, taking its "laah" from the first syllable of Stipe's "laughing." The rototom accents return again in the bridge, which expands on the "in a room" lyric from the refrain. Here Buck plays a Leslie'd riff against a spacey, twangy electric twelve-string riff, also run through the Leslie, but low and off to the side margins of the mix. The placement of this "electric"-sounding effect sets up the drama for the outro, when it moves triumphantly to the forefront.

Now the song begins to build, excavating sounds from the beginning of the song and moving them up to the fore, and switching around established front-stage sounds with a wry sleight-of-hand. The third chorus becomes a half-chorus, in which Bill briefly switches to an open/closed "disco" hi-hat figure, which deviates from the chorus we've come to expect, abruptly truncating it and projecting the song into the third verse with a newfound sense of urgency. On this subsequent verse, a few reverbed Stipe backing vocal accents make an entrance, to contrast with his earlier dry harmonies—a subtle expansion of the song's space.

The Leslie guitar we remember from the bridge gradually rises to the top of the building outro. The campfire guitars also rise in the mix, as do the backing vocals. In the last round of "lighted lighted laughing in tune," the acoustic guitars seem to fragment and bloom forth. Berry slaps the open hi-hat, plays a stuttering snare fill, and moves to the ride cymbal for a jazzy improvised figure straight from the Stewart Copeland drum manual, as Stipe offers a final, soaringly baroque ornamentation of the three-note "laughing in tune" melody. The song ends with a giant strum on the one with a wall of acoustic guitar doing a modified Pete Townshend *ka-ta-chung*, and one final ringing bass note from the piano. It's only here that you might register that the chord hits in the verses were as much piano as guitar and cymbal accent: this piano-hybrid sound was executed like a windmill guitar chord, playing off the unconscious expectation that that's where one ought to hear something like a windmill power chord in a rock song. "Laughing" boils rock bombast down to its structure and then takes it in a completely opposite direction, playing off rock *sturm und drang* to create the same kind of drama in an otherwise carefully controlled song.

Talk About the Passion

"Talk About the Passion" was the second single I.R.S. released from *Murmur*. It begins simply enough, but after a minute or so, you discover one of the song's unusual qualities: an inversion of density between the verse and the chorus. The verse is built around a prominently featured guitar riff, another purposefully ambiguous blend of electric and acoustic fused into one—an important quality of the record's sound, achieved through then-unorthodox methods like miking the electric guitars at their strings rather than at the amp speaker.

The song's chorus, by contrast, almost feels like the floor dropped away: the electric guitars are replaced by acoustic guitars, but they're not "intimate," they're ten paces away. Berry switches from rim clicks to snare hits, and Buck's electric riffs aren't grounding, as they should be in a chorus, they're disembodied. The effect of this sudden openness almost casts the chorus vocal (and title) in parentheses, beseeching the listener: "(this is where a song would normally *talk about the passion*. If that's what you want, go do it instead of listening to a pop song)." There's also a weird turnabout in the arranging of the instruments here: Buck's twangy electric figure on the chorus takes its rhythmic and melodic cues from Stipe's vocal—it's almost like a second lead vocal—but it occurs *on top* of Stipe's phrases rather than in the spaces between (defeating the "call and response" idea more commonly found in pop songs).

Then things get even stranger. They truncate the second verse, cutting it in half, and skip over a chorus, moving abruptly to the "combien du temps" bridge. So instead of the lightness of another chorus, we now get a very dissonant and heavy sounding bridge (bridges are usually fluffy, a place to bide your time as a listener until the chorus comes around again; this song's bridges almost *carry the weight of the world*). The cello on the bridge (played by a somewhat baffled member of the Charlotte Symphony Orchestra) emulates the graveness of Bill Berry's voice, which is probably one reason the band liked it—it fits with the album's synesthesia, where one instrument becomes a strange proxy for another. The bridge is completed by some spacey Leslie arpeggios from Buck.

Then back into the airiness of the chorus . . . and then another, different bridge (!), essentially a proxy for a guitar solo. But instead, Buck plays a very controlled, almost labored acoustic lead riff—it's an austere moment among the "weight" and "passion" of the song's lyrics, this song being the most vocally transparent on *Murmur*. The song ends with a simple but majestic-sounding cello line, which the band dictated orally to the game CSO cellist. "Talk About the Passion" was a newer song for the band, one that hadn't been played in public (it's noticeably absent from live set lists leading up to the *Murmur* sessions). The song's arrangement was extensively toyed with by everyone involved, but according to Easter, it's Don Dixon who deserves much of the credit for the song's inventive and unorthodox structure.

Moral Kiosk

"Moral Kiosk" is a much-needed rocker (in the vein of RFE) after three decidedly moody songs in a row. The song was inspired by the so-called *moral kiosks* on College Avenue in Athens, where students would post photocopied announcements—though others have interpreted the song as a slam on college towns in general and their sheltered liberalism. One acquaintance of mine put it colorfully: he thought the song likened "a course selection well-stocked with seminars like 'Lesbian Pygmies with Black-Market AK-47s' with old copies of *Z* and *The Fifth Estate*."

The song begins with another electro-acoustic guitar blend like "Talk About," but a more full-on, flailing version of the previous song's restrained strum and twang—again, the face of the electric guitar itself is miked as well as the amp it's running through. The chord that Buck is wailing on has a pedigree closer to jazz than rock—an Esus4. Buck garnishes the end of every four-bar phrase from Stipe with some bendy electric accents that are not quite country and not quite rock, but a kind of hybrid of the two. These yawing riffs are coupled with some splashy *pssh-pssh* accents from Berry (the sound of some scraps of oak flooring, leftover from the construction of the studio, clapped together and run thru an over-modulated Urei 1176 compressor, according to Easter). Then into the "so much more attractive" refrain, where Buck's choppy guitar sounds a bit like that of Andy Gill from Gang of Four, with whom the band had toured a few months earlier, and of whom the band were big fans.

The song's chorus is a quintessential early R.E.M. vocal arrangement, a problematic matrix of different-sounding voices and textures that somehow gel and connect. Stipe's staccato "inside / cold / dark / fire / twilight" plays against Berry's and Mills's laconic, almost doo-wop-like backing harmonies—close and dense where Stipe is airy (his lead vocal heavily treated with reverb and slap-back echo), fluid while Stipe is telegraphic. The backgrounds phonetically collapse the lyrics of Stipe's lead vocal, rendering them down to their vowel sounds: *co-old, co-old-in, saa-ade, co-oo-oo-old*. Bill's tumbling tom rhythms seem to stir all the various syllables together until they are no longer parts of discrete words and they slam headlong into one another and burst open.

The second "so much more attractive" refrain now features some tribal-sounding overdubs—Dixon seated the band around a mic and had them slap their pant legs while making the *huh-huh* grunt sounds. A short time later we come to the melismatic bridge, a striking three-part harmony of *ohh-ohh-ohh*s—Berry's moaning voice dominates here, meshing with Stipe's high wail, with Mills's tapering alto poking through the mix as well. The bridge is bookended by a terse electric arpeggio from Buck, a spirited snare fill from Bill, a dramatic descending bass slide from Mike, and then it's back to the lone flailing guitar from the intro (with the ambient room mics cranked up a notch or two) and then back into the verse once again. It's a concise little eight-bar bridge that accomplishes a lot: The sonic texture of the song slips just enough to telegraph that there's more to the song to follow than we might expect, and it projects us into the rest of the tune with vigor—the following verse is essentially the same as the previous ones, but by virtue of the bridge, it sounds fresh again.

After another chorus there's a discordant interlude where the bass drops out altogether and Buck's guitar spits out splintery, atonal chord fragments a la Andy Gill. Berry borrows the *pssh-pssh* accent from the verses, this time synching it with the snare. Stipe is belting out nonsense syllables, climbing higher and higher in pitch (in fact, at one point, it sounds like he's singing *higher . . . higher*), until the song surges into another chorus as the *pssh-pssh* sounds—and Berry's most dynamic drum performance on the album—drive the song to its ending.[4] Or rather, its para-ending: "Kiosk" closes with the classic R.E.M. fixture—the weird, non-tonic hanging chord. The chorus is in A, and the song ends on a D (with the bass line skipping a note to get there), and Stipe's descending vocal line stops one note short, on a B—the sixth of a D chord—making the last chord a D6, a compositionally strange choice. It's a question mark where an exclamation point ought to be—or at least a period.

Perfect Circle

From the relative bombast of the end of "Kiosk"—the rockingest moment on the record between the opening RFE and the closing "West of the Fields"—comes the austere, melancholy piano intro of "Perfect Circle." Berry wrote the song in its entirety (with lyrics by Stipe) and used to play it live on a cheap Casio . . . which didn't always work so well. On a recording of a show from September 24, 1982, in Champaign, Illinois, Buck's and Mills's parts are pretty much the same as they would end up on the *Murmur* version, and Stipe's melody and emotion are all there, but it sounds like karaoke compared to the rest of the set. The band were shocked when they heard the final version of the song, which had been painstakingly assembled for the most part by Easter and Dixon while the guys were shopping at the Salvation Army across the street. Berry's first words were, "You're kidding, right?" Easter remembers Dixon fighting aggressively to keep the version—the song is still a favorite of both Dixon and Easter—and eventually the band came around. It's one of Buck's favorites now, too. The song captures an experience he had a few months before they wrote it:

> The most moving moment I've had in the last couple of years was at the end of one of our tours. I hadn't slept in days. I was as tired as I possibly could be, and we were doing a concert that night for a live radio

show. And I was standing in the City Gardens in Trenton, New Jersey, at the back door, and it was just getting dark. These kids were playing touch football, the last game before dark came, and for some reason I was so moved I cried for twenty minutes. It sounds so trivial, but that's more or less what "Perfect Circle" on *Murmur* is about. I told Michael to try and capture that feeling. There's no football in there, no kids, no twilight, but it's all there.

The opening verse is without percussion or drums. Berry and Mills are playing the studio's two pianos live, in stereo unison, allowing for some great, subtle interplay of variation between the two parts. Mills's overdubbed bass slides in after a couple lines, like in a soul song. On the chorus, Buck enters with some exquisite twelve-string electric guitar washes, and Berry picks up the rhythm of the pianos with just bass drum and hi-hat, and an expansively reverbed snare drum in the left channel that ricochets languidly across to the right, mirroring how the tack piano part has also become more languid and vampy.

On the second verse, the big snare disappears while the hi-hat and bass drum continue, and the ringing guitar sound from the chorus is reintroduced about halfway through, continuing into the second chorus. Then a two-bar pause of just the two reverbed snare hits, with the pianos decaying behind it. The next section is a half-verse; the bass drum quadruple-times to a build with a gong-like cymbal splash, and Easter's spectral backwards guitar fades in—one of the most breathtaking moments on the record, as well as a clever juxtaposition, as it initially has the brassy overtones of a cymbal. Easter's guitar makes some atmospheric sounds before retreating a bit. The song resolves into a final chorus repetition, with Stipe repeating "standing too soon shoulders high in the room," and a gentle fade-out. But just before the song fades completely out, the drums disappear, and Easter's guitar peeks back in as the pianos disengage from one another, and the last audible sound is a smoky curlicue of feedback that mixes with the overtones of the pianos before dissolving into silence. It's the album's most beautiful and mysterious song. It's also Mitch Easter City—no wonder it's his favorite. To go from the throbbing insistence of "Radio Free Europe" to the floaty quietude of "Perfect Circle," from the extroverted to the introspective in the course of about twenty-three minutes, makes you wonder what Side B holds.

Catapult

"Catapult" was a set staple, a fine early live rocker, but it was probably ruined a bit for the band by the ordeal they went through recording the song as an I.R.S. demo with Stephen Hague (producer of new wave pop bands like the Human League and New Order). Hague drove the band through dozens of takes, forced Berry to play with a click track, and then took the master tape to a studio in Boston, where he slathered the song with cheesy synthesizer overdubs. The band hated the results so much that this version of the song is unavailable on any R.E.M. bootleg to this day. Berry was particularly disheartened by the experience, and Easter mentions trying to accommodate him (and the rest of the band) as much as possible during *Murmur*:

I think the important thing about our sessions with them was the fact that we didn't want to fight with them; we wanted them to like what was happening. So, any disagreements were mild and subject to persuasion. We would never have imposed anything on them on the grounds that we were The Producers—I really hate that sort of thing. I think they appreciated that about us, especially after the unfortunate prior session, where they felt like they weren't respected. I'm sure that guy [Hague] thought he was just doing his job, but it's not a style I like, and certainly it rubbed the band the wrong way.

Beyond the exorcising of its bad karma, though, the song is still probably the album's weakest link; it's a little plodding, but Berry sounds like he's finally for the most part at ease.

There is a tiny glitch on the hi-hats behind the first line of the song, which I'd always registered subliminally; in light of Berry's insecurity in relation to the song, maybe Mitch and Don let it go instead of invoking bad memories by insisting on multiple takes. It's the least-adorned song production-wise, which is probably a reaction to their experience with the overproduced demo. Thus, it's the most characteristic of the band's early songs/shows—though absent are Mills's clipped, new wave-sounding *cat-ca-cat-ca-cat!* background vocals from when the band first started performing the song live in early 1982. There are some nice production touches, like the soaring acoustic strum on the choruses, and Easter's buried vibraphone clinks in the "it's nine o' clock" bridge parts. The overall impression is of a problematic song, positioned somewhat pragmatically on the album between its most beautiful moment and a straightforward rocker with which the band probably felt they could do no wrong. In between is "Catapult," which more closely represents the band's early live sound but ends up falling a bit flat in the unforgiving environs of the studio.

Sitting Still

Following "Catapult" is another early R.E.M. staple—its fade-out is suddenly interrupted with a solitary snare hit, either a flam or a delay-enhanced single hit, launching you into "Sitting Still," one of the album's high-water marks. The verses are forged from the symmetry of a call-and-response interplay between Buck's arpeggios and Stipe's lyrics, leading to some muted guitar chug building through the refrain before the gorgeous chorus.

There's a simple, undiluted feeling in the choruses— chiming, joyful guitars, and a loud, instantly grokked lyric ("I can hear you") that binds the obtuseness of the verses the same way that "calling out in transit" is cathartic in relation to RFE's similarly murky subject matter. Stipe sounds passionate, after sounding sad on "Circle" and merely *there* on "Catapult." Stipe's choruses do a lot of different things on this album, but here is where he affirms that RFE wasn't just a radio-friendly anomaly in terms of energy and passion. As on "Kiosk" (the last rocker), Mills and Berry find their chorus background vocals by morphing Stipe's words phonetically—they take the *ah* of a standard backing vocal (back to doo-wop and rhythm & blues, and then the Beatles) and wryly make it into the

/a/ twang of a Southern *I* (from Stipe's "*I* can hear you"). It's a subtle twist, until Stipe finally stretches the *I* into a yawning Georgian /a/ toward the end of the final chorus.[5]

Mills stays close to the bone throughout the song, laying down punk-rock eighth notes, with no walking lines or harmonic accents. Stipe's sound alternates between withering and forceful—you can almost see him contorting himself under the studio stairs. Berry's drum accents in the otherwise subdued bridge (the "talk until you're blue"/"get away from me" part) are a nice programmatic touch: This song is about talking to someone who's deaf, a metaphor that captures some of the band's anxiety, in spite of their confidence and vision, in choosing to make such a oddball record. It's as if the tangible longing at the heart of the song is the hope that in *Murmur*, we can *gather through a fear*, the common fear of not being heard—a theme that relates back to the band's album title choice of "murmur" being one of the easiest words to say in the English language.

There's another sweet drum fill from Berry at the end of the last refrain before the final chorus, like the punctuation at the end of a paragraph, as hoarseness swallows Stipe's last "a waste of time, sitting still"—*thump; thump-thump*. You can hear the semicolon in there, a tiny drama gone in an instant. Then a double chorus, tied together with a brilliantly subtle passing chordal riff from Buck that makes the second repetition feel like a necessity rather than just a reiteration—it's one of Buck's weird in-between chords, with a trace of hammered-on string twang in the middle of it that makes one chord briefly function as another, and it makes the transition work by telling you it's aware of itself, asserting itself in a space that could easily be taken for granted, swept over in the momentum.

A different version of "Sitting Still," recorded at Easter's Drive-In, was the B-side of the Hib-Tone single (opposite "Radio Free Europe," recorded in the same one-day session). Again, the seven-inch version of the song is looser and muddier sounding than the album version, but unlike the Hib-Tone RFE, Stipe sounds strained on the seven-inch "Sitting Still." This is melodically more demanding of a song than RFE, and on the B-side, he sounds tired, as though he's done one too many takes. Here, he's at the top of his game, in complete control even when he sounds like he's about to lose it.

Stipe's final cry—"Can you hear me?"—makes the song's skeletal production values overt. If "Circle" is the album's most private moment, this is its most naked: *are you deaf* (like the song's subject), *or are you feeling all this?* If Easter and Dixon left "Catapult" alone out of sympathy to the band, they left this one alone only because it didn't need anything. It plays as straight-up rock and roll while it borrows the mystique of the album's previous songs to add weight to its off-kilter lyrics and inwardly directed passion. Stipe stretches the vowel in "fear" to its breaking point, as well as his voice, a performance unmatched on the rest of the album, and also a foreshadowing of the next song, which is also about fear.

9–9

Pronounced "nine to nine," this is *Murmur*'s shortest song at 3:02 (not counting the instrumental snippet between

"Shaking Through" and "We Walk"), and hands-down its strangest. The song is an older one, dating back to mid-1981, and it again betrays something of a Gang of Four influence—from the syncopated "disco" beat to the chaotic riffage and clangy guitar harmonics. The song was a live favorite of Easter's, and up to the recording of *Murmur* it was the second song in the band's set, after the opener, "Gardening at Night." It was the audience's call-to-arms, a dissonant blast, and the lyrics about "conversation fear" are the nagging conscience of a choked nightclub. In early live bootlegs, Buck is barely playing any chords at all—this is where the band threw off their bubblegum/garage/Nuggets influence and embraced the jagged timbres of post-punk. Imagine going into the studio and listening to any one of these instrumental tracks by itself, without the rest of the music. You would have no idea what the rest of the song must sound like. If you heard each one in a row, you'd probably doubt they could even fit together as a coherent song. Stipe's speeded-out, logorrheic recitation is almost the most comprehensible thing about the song.[6]

Still, Dixon and Easter found additional ways to glue the pieces together while retaining the song's kinetic energy. A burbling Hammond B-3 organ part rises through the chorus, just loud enough to tickle the ear. The organ is employed for its freaky Leslie vibrato and shrill timbre rather than to strengthen chords, which adds to the song's portrait of confusion—unlike "Sitting Still," it's not the confusion of being deaf, it's the confusion of hearing but not understanding, speaking but not being heard—an interesting compositional shift after "Sitting Still," a song where chords alone go such a long way. In fact, this weirdo track may not have worked after any other song on the record, which is another testament to Dixon's instincts for sequencing.

The only break in the song is where Stipe asks "what is in my mind?," but even this moment of rational questioning turns into garbled gibberish as the bridge melts away into the rest of the song. Notably, this is the song that features the most background vocals from Stipe—he does all of them here. Unlike Mills's and Berry's, they're not true harmonies, but snippets of sound that could be taken from the lead vocal—the sound of the lead vocal's unconscious peeking through, in line with the recitation's assertion that *steady repetition is a compulsion mutually reinforced*. Stipe's backgrounds are indistinct, non-musical, non-rhythmic, somewhere between the recitation and the sung vocals, and then they finally align on the closing phrase: "conversation fear" (which parallels the "can you hear me?" at the end of "Sitting Still"—no other songs on the album close with such emphatic, not to mention audible, lines).

Shaking Through

With "Shaking Through," we go from conversation fear to civic fear: "Could it be that one small voice / Doesn't count in the room?" Here are three songs in a row about communication: First, the fear of not being heard literally (the deaf child in "Sitting Still"), then hearing but not hearing (the alienating social prism of phatic conversation on "9-9"), then not being heard in the political sense of making your voice known, in "Shaking Through." The song builds from the various everyday levels of non-communication addressed in the previous two songs (an interesting irony is that these three songs were staples in their early sets because they *did* connect so well with the audience). This is my own obtuse interpretation now, but in light of this song triptych, it's interesting to take Stipe's odd line "Could this by three be ten? / Order marches on" to mean that for these three kinds of failure in communication, there are ten more that haven't been touched on.

The song's glorious chorus melodies are much more tweaked-out here compared to the straightforward three-note version they sang live in the days before *Murmur*, where everyone followed the same descending melody figure. Stipe's verse melody is slightly curtailed and less "bubblegum" than on his previous live performances, sticking closer to one range so as to better contrast the stratospheric notes he hits on the choruses. Buck is picking out arpeggios on Easter's electric sitar, which buzzes and twangs like a banjo.

With any other drummer the alternating ride and hi-hat on the choruses might be written off as sloppiness, or at best, an inspired jam, except that here Berry's cymbal work adds such a nuance of feeling in these sections it's anything but lazy. It is wildly inconsistent, though—he never plays the ride all the way through vis-à-vis the pop school of drumming where ride cymbal = chorus = apex of song. But it is expressive and deliberate and is a big part of the emotional ebb and flow of the song. If Michael Stipe didn't narrate R.E.M.'s early songs, Bill Berry absolutely did.

Stipe's weaving, multi-tracked vocals in the wordless bridge section braid together and then suddenly cut off, as if severed with a knife. It's as though "one small voice" is lost in a whirlwind of voices that are all variations of the same one, rising to a confusing glossolalia where too many variances on one voice equal no voices, a musical metaphor for the political.

Before the song ends, it modulates up a step, from D to E. It's a fun nod to Tin Pan Alley, but more pragmatically it's also a way, within a song whose choruses are so tightly controlled, of creating a separate, self-conscious space where Mills's awesomely *can-belto* background vocals can carry the song home without undermining the subtlety of feeling created by the rest of the song.

untitled interlude

A necessary palate-cleanser in the form of a short jam, edited with a very 70s ear (faded in and out) and uncredited on the track listing. We just finished hearing the band's three-song manifesto and we need a relatively dumb song now to take it in—this excerpt breaks the momentum gracefully and delivers you to that dumb song (i.e., "We Walk").

It begins with the distant chirpy sound of a tape deck powering up. Musically, the interlude is akin to some of the album's noisier moments—like "9-9" or the break in "Moral Kiosk"—but here it's not grounded to a song, and the difference is the point and why it's well-placed here. It draws on the sonic vocabulary of the album to trick you into thinking, at least initially, that it might be another tune. Instead it tells you that what you're hearing is an album, and should be taken as such, a linear whole. If this were not an album (in the grand old, conceptual, 1970s tradition), but just a collection of free-floating songs, it wouldn't be necessary; its superfluity, ironically enough, adds to the album's credibility as a self-contained artwork.

We Walk

The position of this song on the album seems to say something about the sequencing of the album as a whole. Like maybe a concern on the part of the crew that some of the elements of *Murmur*'s sonic palette that are unusual to 80s rock—like the vampy piano on songs like "Shaking Through"—could by now be wearing a bit thin, drifting into the sentimental territory of later 80s cheese merchants like Bruce Hornsby. The crew's solution is to bring formalist sentimentality to the fore, parodying its heritage. R.E.M. had an affinity for corny easy-listening balladry (they covered Floyd Cramer's "Last Date," and Stipe was a big fan of Johnny Ray) so there's a good chance that this song was somewhat of a joke to begin with. And while the band hated how "Circle" was made into a big production, they probably appreciated how this trifle was made into a respectable little pop song.

The lyrics refer to a couple of Athens anecdotes: Stipe's friend who would trot up the stairs of her house, saying "up the stairs and into the hall," and the shop where you had to go through the bathroom to get to the back room—passing through, Stipe would often see a hand hanging out of the tub, like in the famous painting of Marat's death. The thunderous boom that begins the song (and returns again at the end) is the sound of billiard balls colliding—Dixon and Easter recorded the band shooting pool with the tape deck pitched way up, and then dropped the pitch back down for playback and treated it with overblown digital reverb courtesy of the Lexicon 200 unit.

The song is generally very barebones—except for the doubled acoustic guitars on the chorus, the song follows Buck's hypnotic electric arpeggios. The overly legato voicing of the last verse chord is again a bit of a tongue-in-cheek easy-listening goof, not to mention the fact that it's mixed so loud. This is a where-are-we-going-to-put-it song, evidenced in the fade-out, as if the band wasn't sure where the song has gone, so they're not so sure where it ought to end. There are two rationales for fading out rock songs. The first is when the song has ventured so far, arced so high, that the only fitting way to end it is for the song to stay at that apex and fade down in volume, the upward trajectory of the song mirrored in a metaphorically slow dissolve that reminds you how high it climbed in every moment of its retreat. The other rationale is more polite, a graceful (and easy) way to terminate a song that can't posit its own ending because it never really found its ground in the first place. The fade on "We Walk" falls into the latter category. And the best place on an album for a song like this is second-to-last, where the final song will stamp a boldface period to make up for the previous song's ellipsis.

West of the Fields

A lot of people think *Murmur*'s last track is a throwaway, but I think it's a gem—a concise, exuberant song with clashing textures and inventive arranging. A bombastic delay reverb tom fill starts the song, a by-now hallmark of the album's sequencing aesthetic: the sudden loud staccato sound of a new song interrupts the languid slow fade of the previous (the way "Sitting Still's" lone snare hit interrupted "Catapult's" manual fade). We then hear the patented Pete Buck tapestry of acoustic/electric guitars in the intro. The chorus comes in earlier than in other songs on the album—it's a fast, busy romp, a song Buck once characterized as an anomalous excursion into seeing how many chords he could jam into the space of a three-minute tune. The chorus has a tight, frantic call-and-response between Stipe and Mills in the almost chant-like "long/gone/long/gone" refrain. In fact, Mills shines on this song—his bass playing is spirited and loose (and, dare I say, *funky*), and his "west of zee field" harmonies are earnest and unsettling. Buck has some playful, Zal Yanovsky-like electric licks on the third verse that wouldn't be out of place in a Lovin' Spoonful song.

The song's bridge section (where Stipe sings "the animals / how strange . . . ") is flat-out gorgeous, one of the prettiest on the whole record if not the band's oeuvre to date. Here Berry switches inexplicably to a doubling-up of snare/tom a quarter of the way through like a speeded-up version of the timekeeping on an Al Green record, a soul drumming technique channeled in the spirit of the moment. Stipe's ethereal backing vocal drifts around and through his main vocal, melding with Mills's mournful alto as in an organum choir.

All the elements of the album come to the front of the stage in this song for a collective hand-held bow. The line "dream of living jungle / in my way back home" imagines the Elysian Fields of Greek mythology as the "living jungle" of kudzu from the album's front cover, while "listen with your eyes" speaks to Stipe's synesthetic view of music (he has often said that he composes visually), as well as Easter's and Dixon's technical alchemy. The dreams of living jungle and of Elysian Fields point to a final question in the third verse: "tell now what is dreaming"—more or less the same question that sparked the investigation of REM sleep, the stage of sleep when the most vivid dreams occur. The last chorus repeats twice, fueled by its own momentum, and ends on a dark ringing guitar chord and eerie organ overtones.

NOTES

1. The Hib-Tone version of "Radio Free Europe" is collected on *Eponymous* (I.R.S., 1988). This album also contains the "aggro" version of "Gardening at Night": the same backing tracks as the *Chronic Town* version with a more full-throated vocal take from Stipe, much closer to how he performed the song live at the time. Comparing the two versions of this song shows how Stipe's singing style changed in the studio—and perhaps also how much Easter and Dixon should be credited for guiding Stipe's studio performances: the band had originally preferred the aggro "Gardening," but

were persuaded to use the quasi-falsetto version featured on the EP.

2. Incidentally, the line "speaking in tongues / it's worth a broken lip" makes an appearance in a different untitled song (which also borrows a few lyrics from "Catapult"). The only existing recorded version of the song is on a bootleg of a show at Friday's in Greensboro, NC on January 22, 1982.

3. *Laocoön*: "The priest of Thymbrian Apollo at Troy; he had two sons, Ethron and Melanthus . . . Laocoön aroused the god's anger because he lay with his wife before the second statue, which was sacrilege. Laocoön also opposed the introduction of the Wooden Horse into the town, and incurred Apollo's wrath again. The Trojans ordered Laocoön to sacrifice to Poseidon, asking him to cause storms on the route of the enemy fleet but, just as the priest was about to sacrifice a bull, two enormous serpents sent by Apollo came out of the sea and twined themselves round Laocoön and his two sons. All three were crushed by the creatures, which then coiled up at the foot of Athena's statue in the citadel temple. The Trojans, realizing that Laocoön had angered Apollo, dedicated the horse to the god, and that led eventually to the town's destruction" (from *A Concise Dictionary of Classical Mythology* by Pierre Grimal).

4. In the spirit of full disclosure I'll mention that I'm a drummer—and this is a song that really makes me miss Bill! The decision to credit all of R.E.M.'s songs equally—ostensibly to split royalties four equal ways—wasn't just a matter of the "real" musicians in the band showing *noblesse oblige* toward the guy who likes to

hang out with musicians (a.k.a. The Drummer). Berry was a musical genius—as a songwriter, singer, arranger, drummer, percussionist, and idea man—and the band would not have been nearly as good without him, and they definitely suffer for his absence now. Even by the mid-80s other bands were feeling Berry's influence—one example being how OMD is quite obviously biting Bill's vocal gravitas in "88 Seconds in Greensboro" (from 1985's *Crush*). (Greensboro, NC was a suburb of Easter's hometown of Winston-Salem, and about an hour-and-a-half northeast of Charlotte.)

5. When I asked my girlfriend—who is a linguist and phonetician—about this, she told me an anecdote about when her Wisconsinite parents moved to Texas, where she was born. One of the first things she said was *baa-baa*, and her parents initially thought she was imitating the nursery rhyme "Baa Baa Black Sheep"— until she started making a waving gesture along with it, and they realized she was imitating the Texan "bah-bah, now!" The family subsequently moved back to the Midwest.

6. Stipe sometimes sang the first line as "Nothin' much / right on target," which underlines the song's concern with *phatic* speech: stock utterances that carry no informational value, but serve as a kind of polite social glue, such as *How's it going?* After playing the song at a show in Lawrence, Kansas on November 29, 1982 (just before they went into the studio to record *Murmur*), someone in the crowd yelled "Turn it up," to which Stipe replied, "Listen harder."

III.

The poet . . . may be used as a barometer, but let us not forget that he is also part of the weather.

—Lionel Trilling

I'm of the passing generation that enjoyed music in the worst existing way: the store-bought cassette, a portable circumstance. A brittle extruded product that seemed to crack and break almost as soon as you unwrapped it, felt shitty in your hand, as substantial as trash. It's a medium that almost seems to predate radio in my thinking, a warm smooth backward stumble. I remember everything as brittle and extruded back then.

The cheap plastic clacking sound a cassette made mirrored the fidelity to be found within, or more precisely the lack of. If it were four years earlier I would have had no choice but to buy an album like *Murmur* on vinyl; four years later I would have bought it on CD. Four years later I did anyway. It was my first CD. If you flipped it over, you'd find that the track numbers were printed in little squares on the back cover, so you'd know that's the number you had to punch in on the CD player in order to hear that song. The track numbers were superimposed over an ancient image of a railroad trestle and followed the trestle as it receded into the distance. Each track seemed to number a piece of timber like each was a song, direly so, which makes you think about Thoreau, to whom each railroad tie was a soul—the passing of a freight train was a night requiem to the railroad ties, the sound of a thousand closing coffin lids banging shut in concert. The trays of CD players, I discovered, snapped shut with the same brisk sound with which plastic CD cases snap shut. Tape cases *clack* shut, the way the carriages of tape players and Walkmans clack shut.

I bought a cassette of *Murmur* in a record store in a mall in suburban Northbrook, Illinois in 1983.[1] I was thirteen. My memory of the suburban mall's gilded age has been preserved in American pop culture by various filmmakers as the place where jocks and new waves had an uneasy social détente. Or in the kind of slip-time revisionism that only John Hughes was capable of capturing, a universe where there are *jocks of new wave*, who dump cherry Icees on nerds from the upper mezzanines, like Robert Downey Jr.'s character did in *Weird Science*, which is the most significant way in which the movie was nostalgic to Hughes beyond its camp sci-fi conceits. That scene was filmed in the same mall where I purchased my clacky *Murmur* tape. There was a lot of marble and shrubbery and glass and brass and the mildest of things. But no one really knew what it meant. It was a frontier.

That mall is still there, but now it's just a place where I buy stuff from time to time, mostly around the holidays. Twenty years past, the Internet is suburbia's mall. Unlike a mall, it doesn't matter what you buy on the Internet, but it also doesn't matter what you look like, or that you even show up. In a grim stroke of genius, the stuff you buy and the constructed spaces you haunt in your leisure time finally have the real capacity to transform you into a jock of new wave, as far as anyone is concerned. That's why there can never be a new John Hughes—there's no *place*—that place is now the domain of DSL lines and microwave emanations.

But malls were places of discovery for us nerds of new wave. John Cusack's character in *Say Anything* bought his boombox in a mall, the one with which he played "In Your Eyes" in that famous Cyrano serenade scene that got him and thousands of other suburban guys laid. He stood on the dewy lawn and popped in a Peter Gabriel cassette and a movie about the Chicago suburbs became a Western. The plastic click of the boombox engaging the tape was that of a cocked gun. The real-life Cusack probably bought boomboxes at *this* mall, my mall; he grew up in a Chicago burb near mine around the same time. It's where any suburban Cyrano, fictional or other-wise, would have gone to buy a cassette of Peter Gabriel if one were trying to develop a relationship with a young woman, or maybe *Murmur* if one were trying to develop a relationship with a young cable television.

When CDs were first introduced, people would com-plain about their stupidness. They were round carnival coke mirrors inside drink coasters, and less useful than either. You could at least de-seed a bag of pot with a Led

Zeppelin gatefold LP. The same argument persists with MP3s and iTunes (the Internet's digital mall record shop): there's no music to look at or hold. No opportunity for the homey synesthesia you get from looking at and holding an LP cover while you lie back on the couch listening to the record. Without an Internet, and without access to zines, all I had to go on in 1983 was the tiny reproduction of the *Murmur* cover on its cassette insert, which might as well have been blank. No picture of the band, no liner notes, just plastic and black paper.

I don't know if I saw the "Radio Free Europe" video on MTV first, or if I just saw the *Murmur* cassette sitting in the racks where I had also bought the Police's *Regatta de Blanc*. In any case, it was at a shabby fluorescent-lit store with a full-sized cardboard display of the Journey scarab-UFO in the entrance and rubber bracelets and yellow plastic 45 inserts at the counter and shrink-wrapped Van Halen jerseys folded in black squares in the record bins. One wall of the store was lined top-to-bottom, front-to-back with horizontally placed cassettes, a library sideways.

The cassette was still a relatively new thing. Record companies hadn't yet figured out how to market or pack-age it. Its puny rectangular face was too small to reproduce LP cover art with any modicum of point-of-purchase attractiveness. The logic of retail space concerns (mall record stores in the early 80s were basically bazaar stalls where a twelve-inch LP cover equaled a square foot of real estate) and the fragility of the plastic cases dictated that they be stacked along a wall, their sides too small to project any greater degree of content than the spine of an LP. As a tape-buying consumer, you had to know what you were looking for.

R.E.M.'s label at the time, I.R.S, was manufactured and distributed by A&M, a major label, the better to reach us suburban mall rats. The retail-visible side of the R.E.M. tape looked exactly like that of all the other A&M bands. A cassette of an album by the Police looked the same as one by R.E.M.—artist and album title in unremarkable bold white typeface against a black background. The "cover" of the cassette was a miniature of the LP art (slightly larger than the one depicted on the cover of this book) with a black space-filling void beneath it, the same info reproduced within in the same plain white lettering.

Chalk it up to the fact that cassettes were still an uneasy experiment in the industry, a presumed short-term phenomenon that record companies intended to capitalize on until the consumer tape recorder market went away (with the aid of the "Home Taping is Killing Music" campaign and its admittedly *dope* logo, the cross-bones behind a white cassette skull). Record companies didn't invest too much in the cassette-as-product, because they hoped it was a short-lived fad. Commercial cassettes from this era projected an air of *Okay, tape-boy, that'll be $7.98, come again*. Store-bought tapes even looked a bit like illicit product in their austerity. The tape swiveled back from its clear cradle into a small black box, a graphic abyss that seems even more mysterious now in an age when even the carriages of subway cars are conceived of as viable commercial ad surface.

This lack of cover art, of *information*, was part of my initial experience of *Murmur* and of R.E.M. A gatefold

LP copy of *Led Zeppelin II*, again by arbitrary example, is a geometry of images that you unfold in relation to the music (*Zep III*'s whirly-wheel peep show cover even more so)—a visual and tactile extension of the music. By contrast, a circa-1983 tape of *Murmur* was an object guarded and ambivalent about its own dimensions, its one real image (the tiny cover art) straddling the black gap between the other surfaces folding in on themselves.

And it was one weird image, what you could make out through the cassette pane. The *Murmur* cover broke with the predominant album cover art aesthetic of the time, which was essentially watered-down Precisionist modernism of the type you might find on off-brand tissue boxes these days. The cover art of a band like the Fixx, for example, framed boudoir still-life scenes as a kind of erotic decorative Neoclassicism: Charles Sheeler painting the silhouettes of Scandinavian furniture showrooms by moonlight with a palette full of eye shadow. To the designers' credit, the Fixx cover art didn't have much aura to lose when it was reduced to fist-size.

Still, as endemic as it was—not just as cover art but in all realms of industrial design—the 80s commercialized gloss on High American Modernism always seemed further dwarfed and negated by its presence within *the cassette*—an object that was a much more immediate icon of mechanized industrial production than fake boutique 1930s modernism, and of what modern life was about, and of what you really meant to the band, if you want to take it that far. A lot of 80s album cover art, in its soft attempts to aestheticize the "modern condition," became an unwitting symbol for the music contained therein—a visual parallel to the chintzy sound of a tape case clattering against a linoleum floor. The vacuum-formed cassette case, as tangibly geometric as it was aesthetically empty, was an immeasurably more real representation of the world of factories and smokestacks that Sheeler portrayed in the 1930s, a frame that vastly overshadowed the picture within. Any attempts to dress it up just made it more of a cheap joke.

Murmur looked different, though you could barely see it. The hazy chaos of its cover refuted its tidy packaging while yielding nothing in and of itself. It was like Modernism never happened. It was like a lot of things never happened but finally were. There was no comfy synesthesia, no point-of-purchase reassurance that I'm an 80s dude buying 80s music, in the place to be and the time to be there, friend of the consumer price index and benefactor of a unifying Cold War against the past that threatened to gain on us every moment we let our guard down. There was a blankness and a deep pause. Unlike a lot of memories it was mostly sound. Corporate thrift whittled the package down to the music itself. A purchase was the least of things made that particular day.

* * *

*Japan invades. Far Eastern vines
Run from the clay banks they are
Supposed to keep from eroding,
Up telephone poles,
Which rear, half out of leafage,
As though they would shriek,
Like things smothered by their own*

Green, mindless, unkillable ghosts.
In Georgia, the legend says
That you must close your windows
At night to keep it out of the house.
The glass is tinged with green, even so,
As the tendrils crawl over the fields.
The night the kudzu has
Your pasture, you sleep like the dead.

—From "Kudzu," James Dickey, 1964

*   *   *

When I finally bought *Murmur* on CD, and then vinyl, I discovered a somewhat different story. It was an amazing album cover, inscrutable even up close, an image I'm still finding my way out of. A native Georgian would probably identify it as an overgrown kudzu patch, but as a Midwesterner who'd yet to visit the South, it was utterly mysterious to me.

At first glance it could be a painting or a photograph. It has properties of both. It's organic but alien, like H. R. Giger's art, which was popular at the time, but more like something you'd wander into in a dream, not being as troubled or European as Giger, not on drugs; the kind of post-adolescent dream that signals the progressive blurring of the definition of *nightmare*, a blurring that increases as you get older and you inevitably learn to forget how you dreamt as a child, and nightmares become subsumed as another mere partition of experience.

The lower hemisphere of the album cover makes sense as an electron microscope photo, and not much else—a crawling, hyper-real jumble of polarized fibers. It could be a photograph, or its negative. The intricate contrast of dark and light is like a Surrealist's rayograph of steel wool, a conspiracy between everyday things in a darkroom. When the lights are turned on, what's left is an optical illusion of scale, a frozen surface like "a mass of brown strings / like the wires of a gigantic switchboard" (from James Dickey's "Kudzu"), the opposite of the ordered circuitry on the cover of A Flock of Seagulls' *Listen*.

The roiling quilt of kudzu begins to unravel about two-thirds of the way up, giving way to a darkish blur that only then starts to imply the depth of a natural space, micro giving way to macro. It's a snapshot through a time-lapse kaleidoscope where some facets click by in milliseconds and others in millennia. Nearby is a dark ruin of plant mass that looks like judgment from the shadow of an imploding cathedral. Without reference to the solid Georgia soil beneath, it could either be the remnants of a whole farmhouse or just the overgrown gravestones of its former tenants.

Beyond the ruins, the fibrillar dance of the foreground slows, stratifying into weird sepia tendrils that stretch beyond the top margin. Burnished out like the ghost subjects of a Gerhard Richter painting, the tendrils dematerialize into the colorless sky beyond it, or maybe emerge *from* it. The words *R.E.M.* and *Murmur* are superimposed in the top left corner in lettering that's the sublime blue-gray of a summer evening's dying light.

It's an utterly static image, with a gnawing subtext of movement and drama. Are the fibers eating the forest, or merely providing cover for an unnamed darkness that's about to engulf the entire tableau? Where is nature in all of this, and what is the observer's relationship to it? We clearly see a haunted forest, except it's still alive. Maybe you're the one haunting it.

In the South, kudzu haunts everything. Initially brought to the US from Japan in May of 1876 for the Philadelphia Centennial Exposition, *Pueraria lobata* (or *kuzu* to the Japanese) enchanted the fairground's visitors with its fragrant purple flowers and ivy-like deciduous leaves. The vine had already occupied the imagination of the Japanese for centuries; kudzu figures prominently in the epic eighth century *Manyoshu* poems as a symbol of autumn. But beyond its aesthetic beauty and Oriental exoticness, *P. lobata* displayed another unusual quality that was particularly intriguing to its new American audience: the plant's astonishing growth rate, which wasn't so much an inert quality as it was a full-on botanical sideshow. You can experience the plant's perfumed charms as the morning sun evaporates the dew from its violet flowers, then split to grab some lunch and a nap, and by the time you get back a few hours later, the vines have become longer, visibly longer. At the height of the summer season, a kudzu vine can grow up to a foot and a half a day. One could build a porch trellis in the spring, plant some kudzu under it, and by the end of the summer enjoy the shade of a fifty- to one-hundred-foot growth of vine around the front of the house. Its possibilities weren't lost on enterprising Southerners in the early part of the last century.

Upon exporting kudzu to the deep South, homesteaders and farmers discovered the Oriental vine's further usefulness as a grazing crop (goats and cows love it) and as an effective device for controlling soil erosion. This was due to the fact that the kudzu plant's hearty roots—which can weigh up to 500 pounds—are able to sustain themselves in even the poorest soil, or the sandy orange clay of Georgia. In the 1930s, unemployed men were paid by the government to plant kudzu throughout the South under the auspices of the Soil Conservation Service and the Civilian Conservation Corps, outgrowths of Roosevelt's New Deal. Struggling farmers were subsidized up to $8 an acre to plant it on their properties. There was even talk of cultivating kudzu—a member of the *leguminosae*, or pea family—for its root starch, a nutritional staple in parts of Japan to this day.

The dream began to crumble when people realized the plant never stops growing. Kudzu has a mind of its own. It can scale fences and swallow parked cars and abandoned houses. It climbs electrical poles and shorts out wires; it crawls over railroad embankments and derails trains with its slimy pulp. In his poem, James Dickey conjures up an old Georgia legend when he writes, "You must close your windows at night to keep it out of the house." As the legend goes, kudzu slinks through open windowpanes on summer nights, stealing sleeping children from their beds. The supernatural vine drags them into its depths, the darkness below the fields where the vine has subsumed all other vegetation and the dense, cool ground cover is a haven for snakes. A sea of green where old gullies and abandoned wells lie in wait for the hapless wanderer who attempts to traverse its sargassan summer expanses and falls to his lonesome death, to be discovered come winter when the brown leaves fall away; a ghostly face shrouded in a dead lattice of *P. lobata*.

Kudzu was ultimately designated a weed by the USDA in 1972 and eradication programs and government reparations to farmers were put in place, but by then the situation was hopeless. Kudzu had become "the vine that ate the South," its roots now deeply entrenched in Southern folklore. By the end of the century, the Oriental vine had claimed more than seven million acres of Southern landscape—almost 11,000 square miles.

*　　*　　*

One immediately obvious fact about the cover of *Murmur* is that there are no band pictures on it. There's no distinct band "image" to wrap your eyes around, in contrast to other pop albums of its time. No creepy head shots like Hall and Oates or Phil Collins; no chintzy fantasy illustration like Journey or Rush; no jitterbugging pastels like Culture Club or Duran Duran; and no portfolio romanticism like Spandau Ballet or Quarterflash. In terms of something you were able to buy in a suburban mall in 1983, the *Murmur* cover is the exception to a decade defined by the aesthetic visions of graphic illustrator (and nail salon Caravaggio) Patrick Nagel, the anal-retentive high modernist architecture of Richard Meier, and the unstructured blazer fetishism of Michael Mann (the director of *Miami Vice* fame).

Murmur's cover stands in relief against the sharp, facile, forward-looking graphic aesthetics that characterized much of mass media culture in the 1980s. The photo's sepia tint is the rustic tone of civil war photography, and the draping mass of kudzu in the center of the picture resembles a crumbling medieval ruin from a nineteenth-century pastoral. If it's a slightly Romantic image, it's the primordial Romanticism of Rousseau rather than the decadent Romanticism of Baudelaire. It's complex, earthy, with an almost pre-modern aura.

It was probably the visual associations of the album's cover, beyond any considered assessment of the band's music, that first garnered R.E.M. the label of "Southern Gothic" in the music press. As well, the striking cover of their first release, the *Chronic Town* EP, was dominated by the stony rictus of a gargoyle from the twelfth-century early Gothic cathedral of Notre Dame in Paris. It was easy to follow the dots between the band's neo-Gothic graphics, their dark, moody sound, and their geography, and to locate their ethos under a convenient label. But is it meaningful to describe R.E.M. as "Southern Gothic," as intuitive as this label may seem?

In order to answer that question, it makes sense to first examine what the word "Gothic" entails. It's a term that's thrown around loosely in pop culture, but it has meant different things at different times. In the context of European history, literature, art, and architecture, it refers to one particular group of aesthetic tendencies; in the context of the writers of the American South, another. And in terms of popular music, Gothic of course has very specific subcultural and fashion connotations.

The Gothic sensibility has its origins in the literature of late eighteenth-century Europe, emerging as a dark and sometimes cynical rebuke to the project of the Enlightenment and its liberal humanist values. In the Gothic imagination, subjectivity and emotion override reason. Gothic's foreboding landscapes, malevolent characters, and supernatural imagery represent the intrusion of chaos and superstition upon the modern social order; the revisiting of an inglorious past upon a progress-minded present that would otherwise be happy to forget it.

Gothic's rhetorical and ideological tensions play out in such familiar literary conventions as the resurfacing of a long-buried family secret, the manifestation of an ancient curse, or a decrepit mansion where unnatural events fly in the face of secular scientific reality. The settings are usually remote places, unkempt or untamed precincts on the outskirts of civilization and reason.

And Gothic draws its power by invoking a feeling of the sublime. The notion of the sublime was a popular subject during the time of Gothic's early development, most notably expounded on in Edmund Burke's *A Philosophical Enquiry into the Origin of Our Ideas of the Sublime and the Beautiful* (1757). Burke defined the sublime as that which produces a feeling of awe and terror, a sense of vastness and obscurity that overwhelms the rational mind. For Burke (and later on, Kant), the sublime was experienced through confrontation with nature. In Gothic literature, however, the sublime often functions as a mirror of the vastness of consciousness and of the human mind itself. Kant, in fact, identified the sublime as a human phenomenon, not one inherent to nature—internal, rather than external, and Freud later talked about the sublime in psychological terms as "the uncanny."

The sublime isn't limited to nature or to any one mode of communication or knowledge—any material medium, such as architecture, has the potential capability to invoke an experience of the sublime. A Gothic cathedral, for example, employs sense-overloading ornamentation, dramatic scale, and the physical interplay of light and dark in order to confront the viewer with a sense of his or her own mortality. Regardless of the medium—art, environment, music, or the written word—the sublime creates the same result: a discovery of the self through a confrontation with one's own supernatural origins.

In Gothic literature's questioning of the nature of reality, we start to see early manifestations of self-consciousness and irony. Gothic's emphasis on epistemic uncertainty contains a certain level of cynicism about language's authority of representation—a recognition of language's ability to hide and obscure meaning as often as it creates it. Literary critic Fred Botting observes that "one of the principal horrors lurking throughout Gothic fiction is the sense that there is no exit from the darkly illuminating labyrinth of language" (from his book *Gothic*, 1996). Relating all this back to R.E.M., we see shades of this cynicism toward language in Michael Stipe's obscure lyrics and singing style (which I'll examine at length in the next chapter).

In its critique of cultural convention, Gothic also carries with it the seeds of revolution. Botting explains Gothic's political valences by tracing its associations with the mythology of the Germanic tribes of northern Europe, "whose fierce avowal of the values of freedom and democracy was claimed as an ancient heritage," and who were commonly believed to have contributed to the overthrow of the Holy Roman Empire. Gothic's sublime imagination posed a legitimate threat to post-Enlightenment religious hegemony: the immensity of the human mind becomes a mystical force in Gothic literature, displacing religious authority while subjecting political authority to a higher standard as well. The first Gothic novel, Horace Walpole's *The Castle of Otranto*, was written during a time of social revolt in England at the hands of radical John Wilkes and his supporters, and the Gothic novel was at the height of its popularity during the time of the French Revolution.

Gothic literature was also a threat to American moral values from its beginnings. This is because the European Gothic imagination mapped neatly onto the New World in two powerful ways: through the Calvinistic doctrine of innate depravity, and the mythology of the American wilderness.

Early American Gothic writings—by authors like Edgar Allan Poe, Nathaniel Hawthorne, and Charles Brockden Brown—resonated in the New World in part because they addressed the concerns and fears of the New England Puritans. The Puritans subscribed to the Calvinist belief in *innate depravity*—that all of Adam's descendants are born into sin. Herman Melville observed that American Gothic's "power of blackness" was rooted in the "Calvinistic sense of Innate Depravity and Original Sin, from whose visitations, in some shape or other, no deeply thinking mind is always and wholly free." Early Puritan writings are rife with proto-Gothic references to "animal spirits" and "beastly and sensual passions." And the introspective Puritan focus—one that encouraged the plumbing of the depths of the human mind and soul—were also compatible with Gothic's conception of the mind as a vast and dark (or sublime) place. Gothic's preoccupation with the burdens of a supernatural, malevolent past being visited on the present are in line with Puritanical belief, and by extension, the Protestant American ethos.

The very land the Puritans settled was also an appropriate environment for the envisioning of preternatural menace and doom. The unfathomable wilderness of the American continent embodied the sublime: a mixture of overwhelming beauty and terror. The promise of a new beginning—a kind of rebirth from original sin in a social and political utopia—tainted by the danger, hardship, and menace of an unknown land. Michael Cass writes in the foreword to Lewis P. Simpson's *The Dispossessed Garden: Pastoral and History in Southern Literature*:

> The English settlers brought across the Atlantic an idea, a myth. Whether articulated in verse, fiction, and sermons or borne at unconscious levels, the myth proposed that America was the new Garden of Eden, where mankind had a second chance to escape history. Civilized Europe had failed, but in the New World, in the new Garden, man as a new Adam would begin again. This was the errand into the wilderness: the Gnostic idea of the New World as redemptive garden. The myth was pastoral, in that it emphasized the garden or the wilderness, and it was a myth of innocence, in that the settlers regarded themselves as God's chosen people.

But this pastoral view of the New World as a "redemptive garden" carried with it the Gothic notion of the sublime terror of a wild, untamed continent. The malevolence of the proto-American wilderness was personified in the figure of the Indian—a primitive, animalistic Other that existed outside the boundaries of reason and religious law. Gothic's malevolent animism—talking portraits, levitating objects, the dead coming to life—poured forth from the vast proto-American expanses. Indians were satanic beasts in human form, ruling over a geography that was itself cognizant and anthropomorphic, teeming with ghost Indian deities that collapsed any distinctions between man, spirit, and landscape.

While many of Gothic literature's formal and aesthetic qualities have resonance when compared with R.E.M.'s music, style, and imagery, it's probably important to acknowledge that there are some big differences between a novel or short story and a pop record, as well as in the ways you can talk about them. There are particular aspects of the Gothic mode in literature that aren't very apropos in talking about a pop record—concerns about characterization, for example. But a pop album is a truly complex artifact, one that communicates in three interacting modes: text (the lyrics), sound (the music), and image (the album graphics). A quality of the Gothic mode that doesn't speak to one of these modes can speak to another. I'll examine a couple of them.

The cover of *Murmur* embodies some of the sublime animism of the rural Gothic landscape. Its imagery sets James Dickey's "green, mindless, unkillable ghosts" in a visual array that's both modern and aboriginal at the same time, frightening and awe-inspiring. The serpentine kudzu shrouds and overwhelms the landscape, blurring the distinction between sky and ground, place and thing, earth and that which is on earth. The camera angle encourages this weird ontology: are we down inside of something, looking up? Where is the horizon here, if this place happened to exist and you happened to find yourself there? The light in the foreground seems to come from behind you, or even *from* you, while in the distance light emanates from above, pouring down through the trees but striking nothing. Part of the *Murmur* cover's striking ambivalence is the sense you get that this scene could also be someone's backyard, part of a larger labyrinth that interweaves the urban and the rural, the modern and the ancient, and the anxieties of both places. Beyond the more stylistic Gothic notions of grotesquerie or outright horror, it's this profound ambivalence that defines the image. Tzvetan Todorov, in *The Fantastic*, equates this ambivalence with Gothic's notion of "frontier." Flannery O'Connor called it "mystery and manners."

The album's back cover is a photo of a towering railroad trestle leading up and away, dwarfing the viewer. It almost seems to be shot from the same concave, down-looking-up perspective as the front cover, a way out of the front cover (which is also an image of an abandoned railroad structure, buried under decades of kudzu growth). It could also be imagined as the opposite of the cover image, which would be a shot from the vantage point of the top edge of the embankment, from where the trestle meets the top of the gully, looking *back* toward the tracks, with the tracks coming *toward* you. But it's not—instead it's the feeling of something very old passing by, something that should have long passed by, emerging from its history to find its way into your history, only to pass *you* by. On the front cover, you're stuck in time; on the back cover, you're stuck outside it. The trestle composition is a wistful metaphor of the New South: the futility of trying to hold on to the past in the present amidst sweeping change.

Superimposed over the trestle image are photos of the band tinted in the same indigo color of the front cover lettering. If that lettering is the color of the setting sky, the band members are also diminished, fading out. The nineteenth-century aesthetics of both the main front and back cover images tell you to take these headshots as post-Civil War photography—their expressions are frozen, burdened, channeling not only punk rock's dismalisms (they look like they'd rather not have their pictures taken), but also the defeated ethos of the post-Civil War South. R.E.M. didn't expect their single to succeed (Buck says that they only hoped just to make one great single before they broke up), and the band sealed copies of their first demo tape with a sticker that read *do not open*. R.E.M. was the locus of several different brands of fatalism: the "no future" anti-commercial ethos of punk, Southern Gothic's regional defeatism—and later, the emergence of college radio, itself a kind of turning-away from mainstream culture.

* * *

Murmur's sublime cover art telegraphs some of the Gothic aspects of the music contained within, but it's not the kind of "Gothic" you expect to hear in rock music. The more overt strains of "Gothic" rock rely on sublime reverb to artificially reproduce a feeling of expansiveness and depth in the music (as touched on in chapter two). Reverb is a studio effect used to recreate sonic ambience around a sound source that was originally "dry," or comprised solely of the source sound without the characteristics of the physical space in which it was recorded. In the early days of recording, this was achieved through the use of a simple device called a "spring reverb"—a large box with a metal spring inside whose movement modulated a signal fed to it from a small speaker at one end, and the resulting reverberations were captured with an internal microphone at the other end. The unit's output would then be directed back into a mixing console and blended into the rest of the song to add ambience. With the later advent of microprocessors, this phenomenon could be programmed into a digital module which, when fed with any source signal such as a vocal track or an instrument, could imitate any of a number of spatial environments. A digital reverb will typically have settings with descriptions such as "medium room," "stadium," or "basketball court." To the lay listener these effects are completely transparent and realistic-sounding—though it may just be that these effects are so endemic to modern recording practice that we're used to hearing music sound that way, so long as it's used in a subtle fashion.

But sometimes, the knobs are cranked up for dramatic effect. In Bauhaus's "Bela Lugosi's Dead" (1979), a dramatic reverb is employed, and in an explicitly visual way. The profound reverb effect on Peter Murphy's voice recreates the physical sensation of being in a big stone castle, Dracula's castle. But much as the song is about a cinematic, Hollywoodized Dracula—the song, after all, is about Bela Lugosi, the actor, not the mythic Count

Vlad—the reverb is also caricaturish, a cartoon of familiar modern signifiers of Gothic dread, rather than an invocation of the truly sublime.

Yet bombastic reverb can also be employed so expressively as to be an instrument in and of itself. The gigantic reverb in Schoolly D's "Gucci Time" (1986) is classic and striking, almost the hook of the song. Virtually every track in the song uses the effect, but the snare drum in particular is *drenched* in reverb—it persists so long it virtually fills up the space between beats, the shadow of one instrument looming over the rest, as well as its own.

Here philosopher David Rothenberg's essay, "The Phenomenology of Reverb," is illuminating, as well as poetic:

> Reverb is a phenomenological effect. It works directly at the level of the senses, affecting us before we can analyze it and decide what is happening. Reverb is something that happens right between the performer and the listener. As Edmund Husserl pointed out in *Lectures on the Phenomenology of Inner Time-Consciousness* (1928), once a sound happens, it immediately goes away; and the moment it's over, we begin to forget it. That's what memory, in fact, is: the history of forgetting.

In "Gucci Time," reverb erects a Leviathan of burned-out housing projects, gaping boulevards, and vacant lots—an acoustical decay so gigantic it has its *own* decay. It's auditory mise-en-scène to what's essentially a set piece of inner city Philadelphia under Reagan—condemned dreams of empty space haunted by the sounds of guns, and instead of *boo* they say *bang*, mapping the world's dark spaces like bats in a cave. The reverb from the snare drum creates not only a visceral stage for the drama of the song, but also a correction to the main character's nose-thumbing hubris. It's an exaggerated naturalism—in this case, a frightening urban Gothic wilderness—to match the protagonist's outsized bravado, and it's almost equally expressive. The result is a sonic dialogue that makes Schoolly D's narrative vivid and compelling—the comedy is darker, the triumphs more believable, the defeats more pitiable.

Murmur's employment of reverb is somewhat unique. Unlike reverb's usual function in a pop song, it's not used to build a protagonist, a narrative, or an environment. From a production standpoint, *Murmur* tends to use reverb sparingly and deliberately. When an obviously reverb-enhanced effect is heard on the album (like the giant snare drum reports in "Perfect Circle," or the billiard-ball thunderclaps in "We Walk"), it plays against the context of an essentially naturalistic sonic landscape. *Murmur*'s palette is by and large comprised of "natural" sounds like acoustic guitars, acoustic drums, piano, tambourines and shakers, cello, and untreated or minimally treated vocals. When the album does use electric instruments, they're analog, natural-sounding instruments like organ and "clean" (i.e., not distorted) electric guitar. By contrast, the common timbre of pop albums of the time was created through the virtually uniform use of electronic devices, such as synthesizers, samplers, drum machines, and dramatic digital reverb and delay.

For this reason, when effects are employed on *Murmur*, they're artfully out of place. They beg explanation on a cognitive level, because they don't fit into the universe that's been painstakingly constructed up to that point. The introduction of effects upsets the logic of the songs, creating a sublime tension between the experience of the song as a "real" space and as a space visited by supernatural sonic intrusions.

This sonic tension accentuates the album's neo-Gothic sense of "frontier"—the border where the rational meets the irrational—and baffles any attempts at reconciliation between the two, a no-man's-land that can be physical, psychological, cultural, or, in the case of an artwork like *Murmur*, a little bit of each. If synth-heavy 80s popular music was an avatar of technology, progress, and the triumph of modernity, *Murmur*'s sublime sonic wilderness was a return to mystery, an album of seemingly radio-friendly pop songs laden with secret moments calculated to hint at an infinity beyond reason and rationality, the shadowy edges of the American pop music landscape.

Oscar Wilde, author of the Gothic tale *The Picture of Dorian Gray*, once remarked that "America is the only country that went from barbarism to decadence without civilization in between." For America, Gothic is the language of that dark chasm between barbarism and decadence, between nature and reason. In the early 80s, *Murmur*'s subtle Gothic conceits were a sublime expression of dissent in a decade defined by barbarism and decadence. I had a sense of this myself even before I moved to the South, at which point *Murmur*'s depths seemed to become more brightly illuminated even as its edges began to dissolve in shadow.

*　　*　　*

The main achievement of the Reagan administration has not been institutional or programmatic. It has consisted of a spectacular transformation of popular attitudes, values, and styles . . . In a country where only two decades ago a sizable portion of the population registered distrust of corporate America, the Reaganites have largely succeeded in restoring popular confidence in the virtues of capitalism, the mystical beneficence of "the free market," and the attractiveness of a "minimalist state," even though that state, faithfully attending to corporate needs, has never been close to being minimalist. In the long run, the brilliant manipulation of popular sentiment by Reagan and his men may turn out to be more important than their economic and social enactments.

—Irving Howe, "Reaganism:
The Spirit of the Times" (1986)

When I moved from Chicago to Georgia in the late 80s, battered *Murmur* tape in tow, Atlanta looked on the surface like any other big American city, one point of light in the glimmering 80s multiverse of Nagel/Meier/Mann. Richard Meier had built a big white human Habitrail there, the High Museum of Art, named for Mrs. Joseph M. High (a 1920s philanthropist), but its name could have also referred to the project's High Modernist conceits—an understandable case of overkill for a city with a bloody history to rival that of most European capitals. Michael Mann, whose filmmaking style funnels

American values through those of postwar Europe, shot part of a movie there (the mental hospital scene in *Manhunter* where the cop-hero pays a visit to Hannibal Lecter—himself a kind of dystopian, faux Euro-American—who is confined to a prison that looks like a museum, a quizzical commentary on 80s institutional design aesthetics).

Like much of Atlanta's culture, the High Museum was funded by the Coca-Cola Corporation. Flush with a monetary sugar high after the expansion of global markets in the 1970s, Coke also built Atlanta's largest skyscraper, as well as most of Emory University, a former Methodist college whose corporate endowment from the pop company was up to that point the largest in American history. When I arrived at Emory, Pepsi was harder to come by than mescaline.

The 80s were sweet for a lot of folks, and for those who forgot, their swollen beltlines will remind them like a lipid hangover. Coca-Cola didn't sell soda pop; they sold corn, in the form of corn syrup, a product that greatly offset the economic gap created in the wake of the gasoline crisis of the late-1970s. If plantations laid the cornerstones of Atlanta, the economic reforms of the 80s built its cupolas. The city's mirrored skyline isn't just a paean to Reagan-era corporate optimism; it's also a spectre rising from the sweat and blood of cornfields that stretch to the Atlantic coastline.

Back in my hometown of Chicago, the city's boom era is only visible when you weave your way through the skyline and into the heart of the Loop, where comparatively short early skyscrapers like the Monadnock and the Reliance building are buried in the shadows of their soaring 70s legacies like the Sears Tower and the John Hancock building. Unlike Chicago—the other twentieth-century American city that emerged from a nineteenth-century conflagration—Atlanta's boom era is laid plain even fifteen miles away. From the top of Stone Mountain, the city's coppered-glass towers capture the sun, radiating a sense of the New South, where, through money and media and market expansion, the South remade itself in Reagan's image, his new sense of national pride, much as Chicago had made itself in the image of the East at the turn-of-the-century with the blood of cattle, versus the blood of the slave. Atlanta's skyline is orange, the color you get when you mix amber waves of grain with blood. Coke was a benign world emissary, and CNN shaped its trajectory. It was through this new 24-hour world of media representation, the gleaming prestige of flagship products, and the seamlessly eternal Reagan present that Atlanta found a way of unbridling itself from its dark past over the course of the 80s. Political historian Haynes Johnson describes the new media culture under High Reaganism in his book *Sleepwalking Through History*:

> In the eighties Ronald Reagan and television fitted into American society like a plug into a socket. Together they produced a parade of pleasing images that glowed in more and more living rooms and affected the country like little that had gone before . . . He governed through the eye of the camera and by using devices of the entertainer . . . Reagan was perfectly suited for the role of master entertainer and for fulfilling a public need for reassurance. Unfailingly he sent forth the message that people wanted to hear: Better

days were ahead; national pride had been rekindled, faith in the future restored. News was no longer bad; it was something to celebrate. It was "morning again in America." He was the Sun King, presiding electronically over the new national celebration from the White House. Under his reign, all lines blurred: news and entertainment, politics and advertising. In the television age Reagan was right for America, and America was ready for him.

In the 80s, Atlanta was a crucible of old and new culture meeting old and new money, where past (and current) transgressions are forgiven in the spirit of progress and assimilation. In the 80s, it longed to be America's quintessential Calvinist metropolis, where piousness is measured not in deed but in a Milton Friedmanesque faith in free markets. Where trickle-down economics are the finest expression of the Protestant ethic and the spirit of capitalism. Atlanta was an idea, or series of ideas, made material, much like *Murmur*.

*   *   *

Halfway between Stone Mountain and the depths of Leviathan, on the leafy outskirts of Atlanta, lies the unassuming suburb of Decatur (Michael Stipe's birthplace) and the main campus of Emory University (Peter Buck's alma mater). It's a train stop removed from the center of the city that once called itself Terminus, the last stop on the Atlantic railroad, the place where train tracks and Northern capital ended. It was the furthest I could go as well, the most distant retreat I could find from the stulti-fying Chicago suburbs.

My living quarters were near a Confederate holdout from the Civil war, along Peavine Creek, a shallow brook named for kudzu's botanical cousin. Worn down through soil and clay, the stream bubbled over rocks and pebbles. You could hear it at night through an open window. The house I lived in was a rundown ex-fraternity house planted along the side of the gully; one story spread vertically, like many Georgia houses that transverse the uneven ground. The lower parts of its outside walls were stained the stucco orange of spattered clay. A rail line followed the leafy ridge that ran behind the house, with the creek down in front just beyond the road and woods beyond that. The window in my room looked out at the over-grown railroad embankment behind the house, a scene that looked almost exactly like the front cover of *Murmur*. And at night, when the trains rolled by in the darkness, the sound brought me back to Chicago.

I grew up about twenty-five miles north of the city, in a woodsy area on the outskirts of my town, beyond the malls where teens bought *Murmur* tapes, separated from the rest of the town by a freight railway line. To the east were the railroad tracks and a highway, and the main part of town was beyond that. To the north was one of the last patches of farm in what was once a farming area. To the west were the last remnants of Illinois prairie. The house I grew up in was an old brick Cape Cod on one of the last unpaved roads—the area around my street felt like a neighborhood, but my street was more like a jumble of quirky old houses on wide plots of land. In the daytime, though, you'd know you were in suburban

America—kids on bikes and the *tick-tick-tick* sound of lawn sprinklers.

But at night, the only sounds were crickets in the prairie grass and the distant sound of trains—a low, directionless rumble, like a descending UFO, slowly rising until I could just barely begin to make out the *clackety-clack* of the wheels on the tracks. You'd have to drive a ways outside Chicago now to hear that sound. It was a lonesome sound, almost made of wind—delicate and gigantic, Thoreau's railroad ties giving up their souls to the thick night air. It happened in a place between awareness and sleep, between dream and nightmare. It sometimes seemed to me like the tracks formed a huge infinite circle, and the trains kept coming around at night on their endless trek, going from one immeasurable place to another, and sometimes when I lay in bed listening to the way they trembled the night air it would make me cry.

The patchy road in front of the dorm house wound its way up through the trees toward the campus buildings, meeting the train tracks at the top of the hill where a former train station, mentioned in Flannery O'Connor's short story "The Artificial Nigger," still stood amidst the wild growth of the rail passage.

The conductor stuck his head in the car and snarled, "Firstopppppmry," and Nelson lunged out of his sitting position, trembling. Mr. Head pushed him down by the shoulder. "Keep your seat," he said in dignified tones. "The first stop is on the edge of town. The second stop is at the main railroad station."

In O'Connor's story, set in the early 50s, a prejudiced man from the country takes his young grandson on a train ride into Atlanta in the hopes of dispelling the child's idealized view of the city. Episode by episode, the simple trip turns into a disaster: the two get lost and wander into a black neighborhood, and in their panic to find their way back to the train station, the boy is involved in an accident, and in the ensuing melee the grandfather disavows his relationship with the boy. By having done so, the grandfather's credibility has been destroyed, and as the two follow the train tracks back toward town in their respective horror and isolation, they find an unwitting way back into one another's worlds when they encounter the "artificial nigger"—a dilapidated plaster figurine perched on a fence.

There have been many conflicting interpretations of this bizarre and unsettling story (O'Connor, who considered the story one of her best, maintained that the figurine was decidedly *not* symbolic). But like many of O'Connor's tales, there is a pronounced sense of confrontation—between the country and the city, the New South and the Old South, between generations, between "manners and mystery." The story's Gothic aspects, strangely, are reversed: the shrouded darkness of the rural train stop that opens the story is the safe, familiar place, while the bustling daytime environment of downtown Atlanta is now the alien Gothic landscape, overwhelming in its labyrinthine vastness, and undergirded by an *Inferno*-like sewer system of "endless pitchblack tunnels." Ronald Schleifer observes in his essay "Rural Gothic":

This is where the supernatural is most clearly and terrifyingly encountered—on those *frontiers* between the country and the city, faith and faithlessness, Protestant fundamentalism and cosmopolitan skepticism. [emphasis mine]

In her complex story O'Connor taps the Gothic frontiers that permeate every part of Southern culture, multilayered and deeply founded like the crisscrossing of old rail lines, or the memories of trains that crisscross through R.E.M.'s lyrics. O'Connor felt these frontiers even in the brightly lit intersections of modern Atlanta, being a Catholic writer in the Protestant South, writing about a country where all men are created equal from a region of that country where they're not, a region clutching to its identity in the face of inexorable cultural and political change. And this is what makes Southern Gothic *Southern*: it channels a similar sense of social anxiety (as compared to Gothic's European and early American antecedents), but Southern Gothic's anxieties are particularly tied to loss of regional character, the loss of cultural identity, the loss of the mystery of self. These are the things that make *Murmur* both a Gothic artwork and a Southern Gothic artwork.

In Georgia I heard new frontiers in *Murmur*. A band playing masked pop songs in the melee of post-punk, with punk values and pop aspirations, and a band that harbored more than a bit of the Southern Rock outsider's perspective while refuting its cultural trappings, as well as the blunt way in which Southern Rock bands usually trade on these trappings for fame. A band that, in the video for "Radio Free Europe," projected their own regional frontier—a kudzu landscape like the cover of *Murmur*—onto the electronic frontier of MTV. I felt I was confronting the old mystery of the South as a Northerner, as several of the members of R.E.M. had. I didn't have to venture very far outside the city to feel it—thought I ventured to Athens and beyond many times—or spend time trying to haunt crumbling Georgian mansions (though my decrepit resident house seemed like it could fall into the creek at any moment). This sense of the old-in-the-new permeates the Southern landscape, emanating from the margins of even a tidy burg like Decatur, or Athens, for that matter. The landscape spoke from a deep place, as *Murmur* spoke from a deep place. Hal Crowther writes in his book *Cathedrals of Kudzu*:

> Southern Gothic will be alive—or more accurately, in existence—when the last antebellum mansion has crumbled into the kudzu . . . We don't need marble crypts or moonlight to do Gothic, any more than good actors need balconies and ball gowns to do Shakespeare. We are just profoundly weird.

NOTES

1. *Murmur* was released in the US on April 12, 1983, with the "Radio Free Europe" single following the next day. The album eventually peaked at #36 on the charts, with about 200,000 initial copies sold, while RFE topped out on the singles chart at #78. *Murmur*

was the #2 critics' choice for 1983 in the *Village Voice* and the *L.A. Times*, and #1 in *Rolling Stone, Trouser Press*, and *Record*, though *Murmur* showed up on virtually every other critics' list that year. It was not until 1991 (the year that the band's commercial breakthrough *Out of Time* went multi-platinum) that *Murmur* was officially certified gold by the RIAA, along with *Reckoning* (1984) and *Fables of the Reconstruction* (1985).

IV.

You can write a song about something without ever really referring to what you're writing about . . . You can get the feeling from that experience without ever actually referring to the experience itself.

—Peter Buck

Perfect understanding will sometimes almost extinguish pleasure.

—A. E. Housman

We want our records to be like doors to other worlds.

—Michael Stipe

In the course of an interview that took place some twenty years ago, Michael Stipe made passing reference to an essay that had a deep impact on him. It's what came to his mind when, after having been harangued by fans and journalists alike about *Murmur*'s lyrics, already grown weary from having to continually entertain their broad speculations, he finally threw up his hands. He deferred to one particular document, which listeners can find if they truly seek answers, rather than the easy sport of merely lobbing *Murmur*'s questions back to its authors. "Anyone who really wants to figure out the words to our songs should probably read this essay, then go back and listen," Stipe told the interviewer. "It talks about how people misinterpret something that's being said, and come up with a little phrase or word that actually defines the essence of what the original was better than the original did." What Stipe was trying to say is that if you want answers to R.E.M., you're not only looking in the wrong place, you're also asking the wrong questions.

The essay Stipe refers to, Walker Percy's "Metaphor as Mistake," was written in the mid-1950s, and was later published in *The Message in the Bottle* (1975), a collection of Percy's essays on language and semiotics that would have been available to a young Stipe in the University of Georgia's library circa the late 70s. Walker Percy was more commonly known as a novelist in the Southern Gothic tradition, but he also wrote extensively in the areas of linguistics and philosophy, with the keen cynical outsider's eye of a Southern Gothic novelist. In "Metaphor as Mistake" Percy examines the simple act of *naming*, a profound action we otherwise take for granted in everyday life. Some of the conclusions he comes to are surprising, and indeed shed light on Stipe's abstruse approach to lyric writing.

Naming is a simple shorthand for a complex process: the creation of a symbol. In the case of a chair, for example, the word "chair" serves as a bridge between the idea of a *chair* and the actual physical object to which it refers. This relationship is encapsulated in a symbol—the word "chair." One basic characteristic of language is that words generally bear an arbitrary relation to the real-world things they describe. There's no inherent connection between the word "chair" and our mental image of a chair beyond our collective agreement that there should be one. Of course there are exceptions to this, such as onomatopoeia (from the Greek term meaning "coiner of names"), which is more like direct imitation rather than symbol formation (i.e., the sound of the word "boom" mimics the sound of the thing it describes). But more often that not, words are arbitrary symbols.

In Percy's view, naming is a kind of metaphor too. When we use words, we're naming things, and in naming something, we make one thing represent a completely different thing—which is what metaphors do. Since words are the building blocks of language, Percy then argues that language is intrinsically metaphorical. That in fact language is a system of metaphors, rather than a simple manipulation of symbols, and thus language is inherently poetic rather than descriptive. As Percy explains, "The aboriginal naming act is . . . the most obscure and the most creative of metaphors; no modern poem was ever as obscure as Miss Sullivan's naming water *water* for Helen Keller."

Percy then departs from naming and words, and goes on to examine metaphor itself. He illustrates how some metaphors "work" better than others—that is, they confer meaning in a way that more deeply resembles lived experience. In the example about Helen Keller, Percy grounds the term *water* and the idea of water at the same well-spring: the *feeling* of cold water pouring over your hands. As long as the water is flowing, we don't need to worry about its "meaning." It's only when we step away from the wellspring that *water* then becomes a memory, a symbol. And a symbol is nothing but a way of talking about memory in a way that takes into account other people who have the same memory, who also remember that same feeling of water over their hands. Now we get to the heart of Percy's argument.

By way of naming and metaphor, Percy intends to shed light on a turning point in civilization, beyond language or writing, when the symbol "water" replaced water itself. That essentially, there came a point when there were more people with memories of feeling water than people actually feeling water.

This is the surprising thesis of Percy's essay, and what Stipe probably latched on to: the idea that in modern life—where we have come to take language for granted as a part of our experience—words in fact sacrifice something akin to experience for something akin to accuracy. Percy says the relationship between symbol and object has now become less arbitrary that we might think, and to our detriment.

To illustrate this, he gives the example of a boy who is out bird hunting with his father and mishears the phrase "blue darter hawk" as the more poetic (but wrong) "blue dollar hawk." The boy is disappointed when he learns the real name of this bird known for its characteristic darting gestures: "Although he has asked what the bird *is*, his father has only told him what it *does*." Percy uses this example as a basis to explore examples of similarly evocative "mistakes" in the works of Shakespeare and Nash.

Percy's anecdote about the blue dollar hawk shows that metaphors more closely rooted in the indeterminate nature of words (i.e., the arbitrary relation between symbol and object) create a deeper reality by forcing us to conceptualize and abstract. Which is what *Murmur*'s murky, elusive lyrics force us to do as listeners: conceptualize and abstract. When Stipe talked about "[coming] up with a little phrase or word that actually defines the essence of what the original was better than the original did," he was channeling Percy's essay as it relates to R.E.M.: not only how Percy explained poetry's capability to relate meanings that are otherwise indescribable through everyday language, but also the more subtextual case Percy was making for poetry as a more "real" form of communication beyond its cultural trappings as literature or as art. *Metaphor-as-mistake* is a way of restating Robert Frost's idea that "poetry is what gets lost in translation," or as Eli Khamarov writes in *The Shadow Zone*, that "poets are soldiers that liberate words from the steadfast possession of definition." As Michael Stipe once said, "We want our records to be like doors to other worlds," and, in a lot of ways, a closer look at language is a door into *Murmur*'s world.

*   *   *

Nature abhors a vacuum, which is why *Murmur*'s songs can be so evocative while being so utterly vague. Michael Stipe once described his lyrics as "a blank chalkboard for people to pick up and scribble over. They can make up any meaning they want to." And so you listen, and your free-associative hardwiring begins to fill the songs in. Sinews of connection form amid the detritus of words, connections which then become a private algebra of sensation and image. From this comes a kind of shadow logic that draws you back to a song again and again in the seemingly contradictory impulse of wanting both to embody its mystery and dispel it at the same time. *Murmur* is like Percy's blue dollar hawk: you have a sense of what it *is*, and now you want to know what it *does*.

However contradictory this impulse is, it's quite the opposite of having a stranger dispel the mystery for you, like in pop songs, which is one way in which the book you are reading right now could never aspire to be a pop song. This is also why my book shies from the armchair lyric divination in which some R.E.M. histories have indulged (for better or worse), and from the approach of any other work of rock biography which treats the text of an album—its lyrics—as mere glyphs for the deciphering, a sonic tome whose words are presumed to be too complex for even the most sincere, religious fan to have already heard, or misheard, for himself.

This reductive "Dreamer's Dictionary" approach to rock hermeneutics, after all, was discredited a hundred-some years ago, in different terms, in Freud's *The Interpretation of Dreams*, where the fallacy of dream symbolism's universality was itself put to bed. More so for *Murmur*, a rock album that strikes its fans as a kind of puzzling astral dream if it strikes us at all. And like someone else's dream, I can't claim to know even what Michael Stipe is *singing* on this album, much less what he meant, nor would I put much stock in anyone who does. If this book were about, say, Reflex's *The Politics of Dancing*, it might arguably be a different story. (Arguably.)

To try to tease out across-the-board meaning from Stipe's lyrics, or to presume to unveil what those symbols meant to Stipe when he composed them in the tense pragmatic waking dream of the stage/studio, is to revert to the pre-Freudian mythology of antiquity, which asserts that dreams of *fire* or *animals* or the color *red* always mean the same thing to every dreamer, regardless of cultural context or psychological history. Or, in an equivalent but equally absurd proposition, that they are portents of events to come. Either case is a romantic resurrection of dead ideas and dead books and the long-evaporated sweat of invention of which we think we can still catch a whiff, because, after all, *Murmur* speaks to us. But if Freud placed the divination of the dream outside the realm of civic conjecture, he also made it sacrosanct. The same holds true for *Murmur*'s lyrics: anyone's guess is truly as good as anyone else's. While fandom's sincerity is beyond reproach, occult technique has no place in this parlor.

And on a more mundane level, the interpretation of rock lyrics is a perilous and often embarrassing prospect I'd prefer to steer clear of out of the basic concern of trying not to sound like a complete doofus. In this regard, no rock band in the history of magnetic tape has invited such disaster as R.E.M.

John A. Platt's book *Murmur* is built around his fairly comprehensive, if broadly speculative, interpretations of all of R.E.M.'s early lyrics up to and including the songs on *Murmur*. Here's a fairly representative passage, and a prime example of the folly of the "Dreamer's Dictionary" approach in rock criticism:

> The central question is: What is implied by the metaphorical use of the phrase "Gardening at Night"?—because it's clearly used in more than a literal sense. Generally speaking, any activity normally done in daylight and done instead at night, for no obvious reason, is a symbol of covert activity and pursuant guilt . . . Perhaps as a result of his turmoil, the narrator's gardening at night was fruitless or "just didn't grow," which might refer to anything from erectile dysfunction to a generalized sense of futility—or, to extend the botanical metaphor, the barrenness of the relationship.

Platt must have been bustling in the hedgerows. A lot of *Murmur*'s and *Chronic Town*'s ink blots seem to resemble Michael Stipe's penis from Platt's psychoanalytical couch. If we're to believe his readings, "Shaking Through" is about statutory rape and incest, "Wolves, Lower" is about sexual predation, "Laughing" is about adultery, "Perfect Circle" is a portrayal of "postcoital angst," "Talk About the Passion" equates "sexual and religious ecstasy," and "Carnival of Sorts (Boxcars)" is about "hoochie-coochie shows." I'm not sure if these interpretations tell us more about Stipe or about Platt himself.

To be fair, though, not all of Platt's song interpretations are quite as tendentious as these. His book offers some food for thought. At one point he formulates an intriguing literary/biographical connection from the opening lyric of the song "Sitting Still." Platt notes that the cryptic line "This name I got we all were green" could be taken as a prismatic allusion to Stipe's childhood: a metonymic connection between the green chlorophyll in a *stipe* (a short plant stalk) and the naivete ("greenness") of Stipe and his two sisters when they were all young sprouts growing up. Unfortunately his observation is rendered utterly moot if you happen to hear the line as "This name I got *we all agree*," an equally plausible and popular hearing of the lyric. At which point we're back to divining tea leaves again; mishearing the "open your mouth" lyric from the song "Catapult" as a reference to Opie from *The Andy Griffith Show*—as Platt and a surprising number of other fans have done in the past. Now the mental image of a befreckled Ron Howard will enrich my experience of this song—thanks, I appreciate it.

As I've become less interested over the years in hearing people tell me about the freaked-out dream they had last night, I've also become less interested over time in uncovering the "meaning" of *Murmur*'s lyrics—what Stipe once described in reference to "Sitting Still" as "an embarrassing collection of vowels that I strung together some 400 years ago . . . basically nonsense." Instead, I'm much more interested in coming to terms with how "nonsense" becomes meaning, sometimes profoundly personal meaning, for me and, of course, a legion of fellow R.E.M. fans.

But much as a myopic focus on the particulars can prove problematic, the impulse to abstract can also lead us astray. On the opposite end of the critical spectrum from lyrical sorcerers like Platt, there are the equally ill-advised attempts from within the academy to fix *Murmur*'s red-blooded aura once and for all, to show that *Murmur*'s songs are really just blue hawks that dart.

Katherine Anne Holderbaum's 1990 thesis, *The Sorcery of Popular Music: R.E.M. and the Aesthetic of* Murmur, rises to the task, and admirably so: hers is an ambitious and far-reaching project. Unfortunately for us, she spends much more time wrangling with the theories of Lyotard, de Certeau, Blanchot, and Sartre than actually addressing the object at hand. Her theoretical perturbations seem to restrain her from the ultimate realization that her thesis is in fact another, different manifestation of the doomed condition she's ostensibly trying to penetrate and demystify in the first place: the desire to relieve the tension of an encounter with the sublime. *Murmur* is a record that needs to be completed by the listener, but she has written herself out of the picture altogether, not to mention the music.

The other thing that bugs me about her study is that in the process she also voices a kind of blithe contempt for rock journalists, who are apparently ill-equipped to address *Murmur*'s true import, since their position within cultural power relations (and thus the critical vocabulary afforded to them) marks them as a part of the "sleeping quotidian consciousness" that *Murmur*'s "alterity" so ably deconstructs. Never mind that she relies almost exclusively on secondary, journalistic sources in the form of quotes from old issues of *Creem* instead of primary observation, even as she construes rock writers' crippling "flair for the poetic" as somehow anathema to the concerns of the romance languages department under whose aegis she's conducting her study. It's a bit like whipping the plebes carrying your sedan chair for not running fast enough. Critical theory hobbles itself time and time again in its failure to account for its *own* presumption of discursive privilege—as if ideas could be aggregated beyond the taint of the written word or social conscription, and it'd be funny if the whole thing weren't so grim.

Which puts Holderbaum's project back at square one: Where's the beef? Platt accounts for *Murmur*'s textual ambiguity—its inaccessible lyrics—by not only inventing his own text, but while he's at it, its subtext as well; while Holderbaum forgoes the problem of the Case of the Missing Text altogether and instead erects a giant black hole of even more elliptical language around a seemingly non-existent experience. When you're stuffing and mounting pop culture, it's helpful to remember that taxidermy isn't a type of nature walk, and it certainly shouldn't be confused with big game hunting.

But picking on rock critics and academics is like shooting fish in a barrel. I'm not singling out these particular authors expressly for the doling out of ass-whippings, but to provide examples of particular approaches to explaining *Murmur*'s aura, and their accompanying difficulties. Fortunately, there are plenty of other people who have heard and felt deep things in R.E.M. as well. There's a genuine safety in numbers. If *Murmur* is great art—which we agree it is, since you bought this book—it should not only speak to larger things beyond its simple origins as an impressionistic tableau of something that happened in a small drunk town in lower North Georgia twenty years ago, but also more universal notions.

The phrase "Katie bar the kitchen door" (from which "Sitting Still" derives one of its more contentious lines) may be a Southern folk epithet that expresses impending domestic strife. It may also be derived from the Scottish legend of Katherine Douglas having bolted the castle's back door to shield James I from encroaching assassins. But few of us knew these things when we first heard *Murmur*. So it may also be equally valid *not* to fill in the hazy vectors and missing psychology, not to sift the land-fill of history, but to hear Michael Stipe's language as sound, as I did as a young green sprout—sound beyond language, a corrupted language that by proximity makes all sound language, and makes things without language speak.

*   *   *

Our attempts both to embody *Murmur*'s elusiveness and dispel it at the same time are the means by which we try to account for its core mystery: On *Murmur* there are words and there is singing, but there is no singer. *Murmur* has no *I*. As a young green stipe I'd listen to *Murmur*, and its songs gave flesh to the mystery of the act of saying "I." In fact it still does, from time to time—a sensation of feeling worlds of meaning pivot on one vertiginous letter, and all that it assumes, and all that it conceals. The sleeping quotidian consciousness, as Holderbaum puts it, in speaking as *I*, momentarily rousted from its sleep.

Speaking for myself again, the more embodied that *I* becomes in time, the more intimate my awareness of

Murmur's disembodiment becomes as well. *Murmur* sings of disembodiment, which is why it's particularly apt to think of *Murmur* in dream terms. But just as well, singing is more than a kind of speaking; it's also a particular mode of being, just as dreaming is more than a kind of thinking. The more I speak, the stranger singing seems. I want to invent an equally strange way to think of this. Is *Murmur* being or dreaming? Let's split the difference. Let's make them the same thing for a moment.

Somewhere there's an ongoing scroll of all the words I've spoken, and next to it, also scrolling out, is a transcription of all the songs I've ever heard, one after the other; some of them make numerous appearances. As the scrolls grow, the common ground of shared words and grammar and turns-of-speech between the two scrolls also grows, but not toward any ultimate merging of the two. The more similar they become, the more nuanced my recognition of the differences between the two becomes, and so this difference becomes more starkly illuminated. As I write this book—itself a vain attempt to merge the two—both scrolls grow still larger, and so does the distance between the two, and my awareness of this distance. The distance isn't a vacuum; it's comprised of sounds, too. They're dark sounds. When you illuminate the sublime, you get a sharper darkness.

Back in the beginning, when the vacuum was thin and the scrolls were short, I had an abiding sense that Stipe never sang as *himself* on *Murmur*, even as fictionalized a self as one could allow in the context of a pop song or through wildly dissociative adolescent ears. There was a palpable distance.

It wasn't a literary kind of distance, like when you listen to Gary Numan singing about rape machines down in the park and you know that the narrator inhabits a fantastic realm but speaks as a genuinely human entity who is an extension of Gary Numan who is an extension of you, the Gary Numan fan, with the Gary Numan album, a pop record that you like.

As a metaphor for expressing doubt about the biological basis of consciousness etc., "Down in the Park" is terrific, but as a pop song it's still very literary, and depending on the degree to which old synthesizers float your boat, it's convincing as well. But that's only because "Down in the Park" is alienation making a place at the table for its audience. The distance in *Murmur*'s language, by contrast, is *extraliterary*—a feeling that though there's no observer to relate it there's nevertheless an unnameable something that is *happening* or even just *is* in spite of what few verbs there are to shoulder any movement, and the fact that there is no figure on which to fix any psychology, and the scale is all out of proportion.

Proportion in *Murmur* hinges on that vertiginous *I*, or more specifically its absence. Across *Murmur*'s forty-four minutes the word *I* appears in three places. It figures most prominently in "Sitting Still" and its relatively conventional pop chorus, "I can hear you, I can hear you, I can hear you." The only other instances of *I* to be found in *Murmur*'s lyrics are marginal, peripheral to those songs' narratives; if you were to remove the *I*s, those songs wouldn't change much. In "Perfect Circle," there's the lone *I* in the oblique construction "who might leave you where I left off." The last instance is within the bridge-section glossolalia of the song "9-9" as a part of what sounds like a mumbled "now I lay me down to sleep," but Stipe's voice is otherwise completely obscured in a swirl of guitar and studio chaos, its own kind of glossolalia.

Stipe's lyrics on the earlier *Chronic Town* EP began to hint at the subjective ambiguity contained on *Murmur* even as those songs employed, for the most part, standard pop song subjects (i.e., first-person pronouns). The "let us out" declaration near the beginning of "Wolves, Lower" fixes the narrator in a place, *inside* something. But without the inclusion of the lone *us*, the rest of the song is an impressionistic limbo: "Here's a house to put wolves at the door / In a corner garden / Wilder lower wolves / House in order."

Chronic Town's "Carnival of Sorts (Box Cars)" goes a step further. There are only objects, qualities, and objects bestowing qualities on other objects ("poster torn / reaping wheel / diminish / stranger"; "cages under cage"). The effect is an eerie portrait of a traveling carnival and its sense of otherness. Paired with the distant calliope wash that opens the song (a nod to *Carnival of Souls*, the 1962 film whose score features a spooky pipe organ), it's an evocative and unconventional use of language for a pop lyric.

But the other songs on *Chronic Town* employ more conventional usages of the "I" subject; for example, the refrain of "I could live a million years" from "1,000,000," as well as the otherwise alien narrative of "Gardening at Night." Of "Gardening" Stipe once remarked: "We didn't really write a song until 'Gardening at Night' . . . It was suddenly like 'Wow, it kind of makes sense.'" This is interesting in light of the way the song retains the "I" subject while managing to conjure as strange and unstable

a universe as that of the desolate, subjectless "Carnival
of Sorts." The narrator is present here, and unlike the
subject of "Wolves," is even imbued with psychology: "I
see your money on the floor / I felt the pocket change /
Though all the feelings that broke through that door just
didn't seem to be too real."

It's notable that the "I" songs on *Chronic Town*
("1,000,000" and "Gardening at Night") and the most
overt "I" song on *Murmur* ("Sitting Still") are all present
in the set lists of the band's early shows, judging from
various bootleg recordings. They don't sound that out of
place, because virtually all of R.E.M.'s early songs were
first-person narratives. Some of them are charmingly
naïve ("I fall apart when I hear you speak / Believe me
girl, I just feel weak," from "A Girl Like You"), and some
are just plain stupid ("Baby, I should have held you when
I had the chance / Baby, I could have blew it when I
never learned how to dance," from "Baby I"). Yes, the
same lyricist who crafted poetic lines like "Eleven gallows
on your sleeve / Shallow figure, winners paid / Eleven
shadows way out of place" (from "Perfect Circle") once
penned a verse like "I do the dancin' / You do the hoppin' /
You do the boppin' / I do the shakin'" (from "Action,"
one of the band's earliest songs).[1]

*   *   *

The rest of *Murmur*'s songs—the non-"I" songs—are
steeped in the kinds of things English teachers bristle
over—to be specific, nominalized sentence constructions:
the lack of a clear subject to delineate *who* or *what* is

wielding the verb in a particular sentence. It's what is normally characterized as *bad grammar*. As Bill Berry keenly observed, "[Stipe] leaves out essential parts of speech. People try to guess the next word before he says it, then when it's not there, they completely lose it."

But losing it is a lot of fun, which is why English teachers are bald, stupid, and lonely, and why you can't remember a word of *Silas Marner* yet you remember Stipian absurdisms like "dreams of Elysian to assume are gone when we try" (from "West of the Fields"). *Bad grammar* belies the sublime effects that Stipe is able to conjure with his diffuse lyrics and bizarre elocution.

For that matter, *good* grammar, as anyone can testify, has produced many, many a shitty rock song; songs which take language on its own terms, and so they settle for describing rather than demonstrating, and end up failing miserably at both. This is an admittedly easy target, swimming in the same barrel with the critics and the academics, but nevertheless, it was the context R.E.M. was working against in 1982, so sing it with me now—you know the words despite yourself:

> *I never believed in things that I couldn't see*
> *I said if I can't feel it then how could it be*
> *No, no magic could happen to me*
>
> *And then I saw you / I couldn't believe it*
> *You took my heart / I couldn't retrieve it*
> *Said to myself, what's it all about?*
> *Now I know there can be no doubt*
>
> *You can do magic*
> *You can have anything that you desire*

Magic
And you know you're the one who can put out the fire

The ways in which America's "You Can Do Magic" is a god-awful lyric are manifold and not worth unpacking here, but for the purposes of illustration, it's particularly unsuccessful in light of its bare recognition that we're to expect from it *magic* and *desire*; as a matter of fact, the fulfillment of desire *through* magic. Somewhere between the writing of this song and its execution there's a fleeting recognition of the kinds of terms we bring to pop music as listeners, but it's a warped recognition, lost in the ether between the two imaginary scrolls of experience and art. So, instead of wish fulfillment, we merely get an acknowledgment of our wish. Even within the diminished expectations of soft rock, we'd nevertheless have settled for a convincing evocation of a fictional entity who somehow symbolizes both magic and desire—like, say, Stevie Nicks. Instead what we're given is a passably catchy melody sung by some goober who by any indication is a stranger to both.

So much for good grammar and best intentions. Stipe's fractured verbiage on *Murmur*, on the other hand, is compelling. It not only demonstrates rather than describing, it then disembodies rather than embodying, upping the ante of what we can expect from it as listeners. It *haunts*. Orphan phrases surface in your mind's ear in remote moments, prodding you to decode them. What's demonstrated is the existence of a part of you where nonsense is sense, and that the rest is haunting ground. What literal, worldly sense can be made from "Up to par and Katie bars the kitchen signs but not me in"?

No *literal* sense. But the literal is just one kind of sense. And so you *give* these phrases meaning, inventing hypotheticals to which these fragments refer, proxied notions looking for passage to the world of real things. Somewhere in the whole melee you become aware that non-meaning also bestows a kind of meaning. By this logic, non-meaning exists in some finite place. Then you found this place, and in the process your trajectory was obliterated along with the proposition that beckoned you to follow it. Now you're orphaned like a phrase, floating between scrolls. What you're left with is not only the sense that *Murmur* communicates across a distance, but that the very distance itself seems to communicate.

Still, R.E.M. can't be too weird. R.E.M. is pop music. But *can't* is a tricky qualifier. If someone says "you can't take too many vitamins," does it mean that it's inadvisable to take too many vitamins, or that there's no such thing as taking too many vitamins? Pop music is also a kind of *can't*, a weird mineral. It's sometimes difficult to gauge just how much weirdness we're ingesting.

Like vitamins, *Murmur* tastes weird. *Murmur* communicates across a distance where the distance itself seems to communicate. But pop music is *about* distance; pop music isn't necessarily cold, and distance itself isn't necessarily cold.

The bare fact that we can recognize distance and talk about it demonstrates its place in the lexicon of earthy experience. The greater part of contemporary musical experience, for that matter, has already been translated and (p)recontextualized before we even enter the picture.

It's understandable, then, that we can live this distanced experience of music every day without quite knowing how it happened, or that it even happened. Left unchecked, we end up with soft rock, where the idea of magic supplants magic and the idea of desire quenches desire.

So we start with earthy mineral fact, before pop music made us swallow cold strange things. For most of history, up until very recently, music was heard only when it was performed. In the Hellenic age, traveling poets told stories to the song of a lyre. In eighteenth century Europe, there was the parlor recital. In the pre-Civil War South, there was the field holler and the ring shout; later came rural blues, country brass bands, and the spiritual. These musical genres were steeped in first-hand experience, if not in fact full-fledged collective participation. Any non-performance-based conception of music, like "the music of the spheres," was purely metaphorical, and was recognized as such, in a world that Walker Percy might argue we've fallen from.

Then the radio age arrived. Where you would have once attended a concert, listening to the performance with maybe a libretto in your lap to refer to, now you sat at home in front of a radio or a phonograph. Electricity changed music in the twentieth century the same way the printing press changed the spoken word in the fifteenth century. The advent of plastics and the long-playing album began to objectify our conception of music, transforming it from real experience to a document of experience. Music became object-oriented, something inscribed on a surface that you could buy and own and move from one place to another—essentially, another text to be read.

Though rock obviously has its antecedents in "folk" (i.e., performative, spoken-word) traditions, rock is also the first musical genre born to the age of music-as-text, where its experience is always at varying levels of remove from its point of creation; in fact, defined by these levels of remove, in many ways. It's virtually impossible to talk about even the earliest days of rock and roll without also talking about its media, be it the vinyl record or the radio.

This crucial shift—brought on by recording technology—in the necessity to apprehend musical performance as a first-person observer, also gave rise to a subtle kind of doubt. A lot more people had access to rock music, as compared to any other single musical movement in history, but this cultural mobility also made rock second-hand from the get-go, always a degree of separation from the performance (or other communicative act) at its core.

It's still happening. When we go to check out a band that has piqued our curiosity, performing at the local indie-rock beer dive, they're more often than not judged in relation to how we first heard them on a recording. Conversely, if we encounter a previously unfamiliar band through an amazing live show, but are then let down upon hearing their record, not only does the recorded version of the band have equal value in our estimation, the recording might cast our opinion of them as a *crappy band*, despite our first-hand experience.[2]

The structural distance that's endemic to our experience of rock is then, perplexingly, part of the measure of its authenticity. What was once a mere analog of *the aesthetic* as Plato or Aristotle would have conceived of it is not only an aesthetic in and of itself now, it's the more important one, the *real* one. This is pop music's distance, the fountainhead of its weirdness. Then language further complicates things by populating the landscape of this abyss with voices in song that seem to speak as much *against* this distance as *from* it.

With that said, the distance in *Murmur*'s language is a slightly different animal, deeper than with most pop bands, yet somehow more engaging for its unfamiliarity. *Murmur* has a particularly warm distance that differs from other pop albums of its time, vacuum-formed pop baubles that are nevertheless sung *by* a specific person *to* a specific person *with* a specific person in mind to hear it and make it all "real" in the end, on the other side of the abyss . . . *you*. If distance is implicit in pop music's phenomenology, then there's something else to *Murmur*'s songs, a kind of tension outside of the divorce between artist and audience. It's the tension in hearing a song sung and not really knowing whose song it is—the singer's, the subject's, yours? Someone, or something, else's? This tension is as familiar as the distance, a part of the distance, but it's more at home in the realms of literature and real life than it is in a rock song, and it's what gives *Murmur*'s communicative powers their extraliterary aura.

*   *   *

Just as it's hard not to think about rock music without thinking in terms of its media, it's also difficult to talk about music at large without addressing its similarly entangled relationship with literature.

Western art music, in general terms, is about the per-formance of characters in the context of a narrative, as in operatic song. By contrast, the innovation of the blues is in the composer finally representing *himself* in song, speaking as an authentic first-person. Rock music, by way of pedigree, tends to follow the blues principle of "expression" as its defining aesthetic, favoring authentic performance over skilled interpretation of repertoire. *Murmur*'s core mystery—its "lack of a singer"—derives from the fact that Michael Stipe does neither. In *Murmur*'s songs, there *are* no characters, and no authors; no authentic first-person and no character in a narrative. Without characters or an authorial voice, there's no self—no *I*.

This could be seen from the modern end of things as a kind of nihilistic gesture, an artistic attempt at conveying a kind of negation of self. In light of R.E.M.'s avowed punk rock influences, it's not an unreasonable assumption. But to ground this particular viewpoint in the context of two of Stipe's earliest influences from punk rock—the New York Dolls and Wire—Stipe's vocal aesthetic is the difference between, on the one hand, the egocentric nihilism of the Dolls (who definitely had a "singer"), and on the other hand, the nothing-exists-anymore-if-it-ever-existed shade of nihilism which Wire exuded.

As far as rock bands go, merely having influences is a foregone conclusion—some might argue that rock is *about* appropriation, or even misappropriation—but as-signing calculation in mediating those influences is an-other thing—and when people disparage bands in terms of their influences, they're really talking about the singular influence of calculation. But there's some pretty good evidence here in the form of widely available bootleg recordings of R.E.M.'s performances up until the time of *Murmur* from which we can judge the slippery notion of influence, at least in terms of Stipe's vocal performance, and some of them are so embarrassing, you can *bet* the band didn't figure that anyone had a tape recorder in their pocket that night.

In terms of the evolution of Stipe's lyrics, these two poles (the Dolls and Wire) correspond respectively to the pre-*Murmur* Stipe—

—who in R.E.M.'s early days wrote songs about relationships between people where one person is the object (an essentially Romantic sensibility, compatible with the Dolls' debased "love songs" and fetishistic sense world)

—and the subsequent *Murmur*-era Stipe, who removed himself from his lyrics altogether in service of *the idea of relationship*, in a structural sense.

Or, in other words, what's left when *everything* is an object, and all vectors that would normally indicate agency and causality (the operators between the variables, in math parlance) are stripped away. Stipe's lyrics on *Murmur* are a profound, if perhaps unwitting, experiment in pop lyric pragmatics. Stipe's ultimate abandonment of his early David Johansen influence ought to indicate how much value he assigned to the ego-fueled, and ultimately self-contradictory, brand of punk nihilism.

In this regard, Wire's bearing on the language of *Murmur* is worth examining. Wire, being a rock band, ought to have followed the expressionist blues principle in some fashion, by virtue of rock's cultural and artistic lineage with the blues. In one formulation, it might be some kind of variation on the idea of the "signifier" from African-American mythology. The archetype of "signifier" is manifested in urban electric blues (or "Chicago" blues) in the role of a member of the band without a microphone who backs up the version of events offered by the singer through barely audible *uh-huh*s and *yeah!*s (as in Muddy Waters' "Mannish Boy" and its innumerable pop variants).

But beyond being a rock band, Wire was also a punk band. Punk rock's innovation, in a nutshell, was to put the signifier up front, in effect defeating pop's narrative distance—"out-bluesing," in a sense, both rock and blues itself. With punk rock, not only does the signifier now have a microphone, but he's backing up his own version of events. He's the singer as well as the guy who can't sing but who nevertheless feels what the singer is doing so strongly that he thinks you ought to hear him too.

But punk's innovation, in this sense, was a hollow one. As punk became familiar to wider audiences, its signifying became just another kind of musical material, another Western mode of hearing a character in a song. Thus it lost its connection with authenticity and became rhetoric, a voice divorced from the feeling of the music, another kind of pop distance. The genius of Wire was their ability to acknowledge and express, within the very context of a punk band, punk's ultimate inability to break down this wall of communication. Their songs address the role that perspective plays in the way pop songs mediate the distance between reality and art, the "signifier" and the

fictional pop song character. Julian Cope offers this suc-
cinct description of Wire's 1977 debut album *Pink Flag*:

> Like Magritte's enigmatic paintings, everything is tidy
> and accounted for, but something is still . . . not right.
> [Wire] took punk and twisted it into an uneasy art
> form, stripped it down further and adding oblique yet
> matter-of-fact subject matter so mundane and pre-
> sented without bias, framing or oftentimes, key refer-
> ence points, that the musical portraits fill themselves
> in by default of insinuation and the merest hint of
> conjecture. And most of them bear an observer point
> of view, but one whose eye is constantly drawn to
> detail, which creates an unintentionally skewered take
> on the events he's witnessed.

Wire refined this stripping-down of the narrative voice
on subsequent albums like *Chairs Missing* and *154*, gradually approaching a point where the observer begins to
dissolve into the mechanics of observation, and finally
into the mists of language. In the paranoid anti-narrative
of Wire's "The 15th" (from their 1979 album *154*), language itself is called into question not only for its culpabil-
ity in shaping reality, but in corrupting the arbiters of
reality as well. Subject and object merge and become
indistinguishable, circumstance becomes motive and then
evidence, while nominative grammar single-handedly
brings a sublime threat into being (as well as an English
teacher's nightmare). This was England at the cusp of
the Thatcher era, so it's not going to sound like Little
Richard:

Reviewed it seemed as if someone were watching over it
Before it was as if response were based on fact

Providing / Deciding / It was soon there
Squared to it / Faced to it / It was not there

Renewed it fought as if it had a cause to live for
Denied it learned as if it had sooner been destroyed

Providing / Deciding / It was soon there
Squared to it / Faced to it / It was not there

Reviewed it fought as if someone were watching over it
before it had sooner been denied
Renewed it seemed as if it had a cause to live for
Destroyed it was later based on fact

Providing / Deciding / It was soon there
Squared to it / Faced to it / It was not there

The second half of each chorus ("Squared to it / Faced to it / It was not there") seems to imply that the true nature of the *thing* to which the song continually alludes was eventually uncovered, but that its uncovering was stillborn for the fact that *it* could still only be communicated through the Leviathan of pseudo-bureau-speak. "It" was never to be revealed, the triumph of its discovery evaporated into clouds of lingua franca, a mutual conspiracy necessary for each party's continued sustenance. Wire turns the expected climax of the chorus into a meditative anticlimax.

Maybe it would be valuable at this point to think about what a chorus is *supposed* to do. The word *chorus* comes to us originally from Greek tragedy. A chorus in a Greek play wasn't a section of a song—at least not in the modern, pop sense as we understand it—though it was usually comprised of a group of people singing together. Later religious music from the Middle Ages on appropriated the Greek etymology, but only to describe a group of singers strictly in terms of a musical material to be employed compositionally, losing some of the word's original implications.

What's worth remembering is that the Greek *chorus* was also a dramatic device attached to a physical place in the amphitheater, usually the orchestra area between the stage and the audience. As in its modern usage, the chorus was sung, and it often recapitulated events from the play's narrative, but most importantly, it served to emphasize the idea of *speaking-outside*, or metanarrative; oftentimes within plays the protagonist would break character from time to time (in a section called the *parabasis*) in order to deliver wisdom from outside the play's narrative.

> The Chorus rejoiced in the triumph of good; it wailed aloud its grief, and sympathised with the woe of the puppets of the gods. It entered deeply into the interest of their fortunes and misfortunes, yet it stood apart, outside of triumph and failure . . . No gladness dragged it into the actual action on the stage, and no catastrophe overwhelmed it . . . It was the ideal spectator, the soul being purged, as Aristotle expressed it, by Pity and Fear, flinging its song and its cry among the passions and the pain of others. It was the "Vox Humana" amid the storm and thunder of the gods. (Lauchlan Maclean Watt, *Attic and Elizabethan Tragedy*, 1908)

Dramatic devices like the *chorus* and the *parabasis* were born of the democratic atmosphere of historical Greece, and the paramount idea that there are always other perspectives outside of the attendant one (mirroring the blues idea of the signifier). By comparison, the chorus of Wire's "The 15th" subverts this idea of *speaking-outside*: the song's internal narrative has in effect hijacked the chorus, ventriloquized it, submitted it to its own terms.

Murmur contains this same sense of struggle—who gets to speak, and who gets to hear—but it's something like the opposite side of the same coin. If "The 15th" is a case study in language's potential for sociopolitical entrapment, *Murmur* is a case study in how to escape it. Where the language of song once provided an arena for the struggle between the self and its context, in *Murmur*, language itself is now called into question. In *The Prison-House of Language*, Fredric Jameson explains the importance of such a distinction:

> The deeper justification for the use of the linguistic model or metaphor . . . lies in the concrete character of the social life of the so-called advanced countries today, which offer the spectacle of a world from which nature has been eliminated, a world saturated with messages and information, whose intricate commodity network may be seen as the very prototype of a system of signs. There is therefore a profound consonance between [the investigation of language] and that systematized and disembodied nightmare which is our culture today.

Wire's "The 15th" appropriates the mechanics of corporate-speak and government double-talk in order to illustrate language's social power, and thus its potential as an instrument of control. In doing so, it makes reference to the "systematized and disembodied nightmare" that is the current state of affairs, mirroring the era that produced such press conference damage-control gems as "Mistakes were made," and "It depends on what the meaning of the word 'is' is." "The 15th" is a demonstration of how discourse (verse) can be subsumed by political/cultural context (chorus). Likewise, the essentially neo-Gothic sense of the duplicity of language evidenced on *Murmur* is also a kind of reaction: a reaction to a media-driven, language-fueled epoch where meaning is expected to be crystal-clear and immediate, or failing that, maddeningly opaque. It's significant that R.E.M. would eventually revisit Wire's derangement of narrative through their cover of *Pink Flag*'s "Strange" on what would be their most explicitly political album to date, 1987's *Document*.

It's this aspect that gives *Murmur*'s poetics their political valence. Its tension between *voice* and *author* acknowledges the specter of doubt we feel from time to time about who or *what* is really speaking when anyone tells us anything. It harbors a ghost of cynicism about language's validity as a technology (as it is sometimes referred to), cynicism about the very forces that made language so indispensable in the first place that we not only take its powers for granted, but that we would presume it on the level of something as mundane and dutiful as a *tool*, a device to perform a task reliably and unequivocally. A tool, after all, is a thing that does what it's told as though it were a limb of our body rather than another soft tendril of the mind.

But technology can also be man's idle hand, with potential for abuse. The Reagan years, which formed the backdrop to *Murmur*, saw an age where politicking expanded the realm of the spoken word as a form of weaponry. Speaking softly became its own big stick, a proxy for the Soviet pageantry of tank colonnades and missile floats in Red Square. And like technology, language also can escalate and get away from us, where words become so meaningless we need to bring out the things they refer to, the ICBMs and the MIRVs. In the 80s, Americans began to feel the power of language metastasizing into something else, the power of terror and fear. They wanted to stop the escalation before it was too late. They wanted to disarm language, or, failing that, divest themselves of it. How would you execute such a task when your only context is pop culture, which relies on your power in terms of economics, but which grants you none in return? You can't. You can only imagine it.

Until something comes along that causes you to suspect that maybe others are imagining it, too, and, without words, offers a tactic. The tactic, as Peter Buck says, is to "short-circuit the whole idea that literal language is what things are, because literal language is just code for what happens." This is why *Murmur*, which in all respects seemed to contradict everything about its cultural context, nevertheless seemed to fit it like a glove. This contradiction was not only right, it became a new context that swallowed the current one. It could kill the person who has taken it upon himself to ghostwrite our page of history.

The most direct way to short-circuit language, as Buck put it, is to short-circuit the author. This is what Stipe does by concealing the agents of his songs' narratives. I use the word *narrative* partially for lack of a better word, but also because the forward momentum of a pop song has a way of imposing narrative on even the most obtuse (or in certain cases, inept) lyrics—a teleological sense of movement from some starting point to some kind of end roughly three-and-a-half minutes later. Even the obtuse anti-narratives of *Murmur* have an underlying drama. Susan McClary observes in her article "The Impromtu that Trod on a Loaf: or How Music Tells Stories":

> It is important to recall that during the nineteenth century virtually all cultural enterprises in Europe aspired to the condition of narrative, whether historiography, philosophy, biology, political science, painting, or psychoanalysis. As theorists such as Ricoeur and Hayden White explain, narrative allows for the introduction, interaction, and eventual resolution of apparently incompatible elements within a unified process, and practitioners within all these enterprises found such a dynamic, though ultimately stable, pattern extremely satisfying. Not surprisingly, this totalizing habit of cultural thought—which may be more evident to us in retrospect than those in its thrall—also informed musical procedures.

She continues:

> But it is easier to perceive this ideology when our expectations are frustrated—when, in other words, *a*

piece fails or refuses to work as the contract guarantees.
Not only does it tread on a loaf and suffer the conse-
quences, but its descent into hell gives us a perspective
from which to interrogate the everyday world of ge-
neric musical norms. [emphasis mine]

It's odd that there is any drama to be had on *Murmur*,
given the fact that Stipe's non-characters are also working
with non-verbs, or more properly, passive verb constructions. They're ghosts with ghost guns, and when they
go off, they barely make a sound. Choruses which by
conventional definition should resound with a feeling of
immediacy—the Aristotelian "pity and fear" of the verses
packed into a small space and detonated—are instead
static ransom-notes of gerunds. There's the "Lighted,
lighted, laughing in tune" refrain from "Laughing" (which
echoes the "Providing, deciding" chorus of Wire's "The
15th"). And of course there's the classic "Calling out in
transit" line in "Radio Free Europe." These anti-choruses
stand in stark opposition to the Greek idea of chorus as
metanarrative, something that explains the narrative by
imposing context.

Instead, in his choruses Stipe frames the act itself by
blacking out the actor altogether. Another term for *ger-
und*, after all, is *verbal noun*—an action made into an
object. In "Perfect Circle," it's "Standing too soon, shoulders high in the room." In "Shaking Through," it's just
"shaking through" plus the free-floating token "opportune"—situated as though to qualify things, which it
doesn't. In "Moral Kiosk," the chorus is devoid of action
altogether—a sentence fragment, or fragments, de-

pending how you parse it: "Inside / cold / dark / fire / twilight."

Devoid of the mechanics with which to complete themselves, these images stall in your mind—or more specifically, the words stall long enough to become images. This is Stipe the visual artist, conceiving of song lyrics like moving pictures, where images can be shuffled in succession to create movement, or merely repeated unchanged. Both modes have equal weight, since in film even static shots are comprised of movement—the opposite of language, where the movement of the physical world is frozen in code and symbol. We barely register moments in movies when one stationary image persists on screen for an extended moment. In a pop song, that same stasis is arresting. "I also have slow motion and stop action and black and white and color," says Stipe. "I always see it before I hear it."

*   *   *

As abstract as Stipe can get, he nevertheless always refers to the real world, the apparent world; and as a visually oriented lyricist, his metaphorical worlds harbor vivid resonances of the physical world. Percy's *metaphor-as-mistake* also connects one visual aspect of R.E.M.'s songwriting—its vision of the pastoral—with another earlier visionary of the American pastoral consciousness, Henry David Thoreau. Literary critic Barbara Johnson explains Thoreau's collapsing of metaphor in *Walden*:

> The perverse complexity of *Walden*'s rhetoric is intimately related to the fact that it is never possible to

be sure what the rhetorical status of any given image is. And this is because what Thoreau has done in moving to Walden Pond is to move *himself*, literally, into the world of his own figurative language. The literal woods, pond, and bean field still assume the same classical rhetorical guises in which they have always appeared, but they are suddenly readable in addition as the nonfigurative ground of a naturalist's account of life in the woods. The ground has shifted, but the figures are still figures . . . *Walden* is obscure, therefore, to the extent that Thoreau has *literally* crossed over into the very parable he is writing, where *reality itself* has become a catachresis, both ground and figure at once . . .

Thoreau's mixed, overextended, and incomplete metaphors are precisely the kinds of "mistakes" Percy talks about in his essay: a way of overcoming language's role in the "spectacle of a world from which nature has been eliminated," as Jameson says. Peter Buck has made similar statements about R.E.M.'s language: "We decided that we ought to take all these clichés and mutate them. Take fairy tales, old blues phrasings, clichés . . . and just twist them so they were evocative but skewed and more resonant." Author Robert W. Rudnicki, in his book *Percyscapes*, further articulates how *metaphor-as-mistake* can be a tactic for breaking out of the culturally enforced, Jamesonian prison-house of language:

When a language becomes highly phatic [i.e., polite rather than meaningful] and scripted, when the code and channel of discourse are privileged to the detriment of the message, then, Percy argues, the users of that language become as hollow, dead, and feckless as their discourse. In other words, the inability to use language authentically is, argues Percy, symptomatic of a larger psychological ailment.

*　　*　　*

Still, some scientists of the word travel the furthest folds of the human sphere to try and uncover more pristine outposts of culture with which to disprove the kinds of possibilities that Thoreau and Percy—and Stipe—imagined. Of course, they already had a name in mind for what they had yet to discover. It was *linguistic relativity*—the theory that holds that thoughts are determined by the language available to express them, that one cannot formulate what exists outside the boundaries of language. It would follow that an utterance without a linear meaning is at best poetic, at worst gibberish, even though you and I knew otherwise at the age of thirteen, in the dark with R.E.M. coming through our headphones.

When you listen to *Murmur* it makes sense that Walker Percy's ideas resonated with Stipe. But they probably just confirmed the poetic sensibility Stipe had already been developing, the sense of the elusive powers of language not only to relate commonly understood meanings but also to create meanings that only exist in language and symbol—in Percy's words, "an inscape familiar to one and yet an inscape in bondage because I have never formulated it and it has never been formulated for me."

But it's also safe to assume that Stipe began obscuring the subjects of his songs at least partially as a device to circumvent pop song clichés—*x* does *y* because of *z*. The tension I mentioned earlier in this chapter—the tension beyond pop's implicit distance—is Stipe pushing against the boundaries of linguistic relativity to escape ego and the idea of universal symbolism that Freud argued against, and the way it supposes ego in the realm of rock lyric cliché—that instead of having words that move like blue darts, we have songs about things that dart and are blue.

But they're clichés, of course, because they work. People project themselves into pop songs; it's their appeal if not their *raison d'être*. But part of projecting yourself into a pop song is the tacit notion that you're able to momentarily leave behind the reality and the narrative you normally inhabit. That may or may not even be possible, but if it is, *Murmur*'s songs are those discarded clothes, the persona without the animus. By seemingly dislocating himself—Michael Stipe—from the voice performing the song, he defeats the ego of the singer-subject, abstracting the events of the lyrics to anyone. The sweet edge dividing you through the heart and marrow. The place where pop sheds its skin.

All told, Stipe is an intriguing language artist, but it would be irresponsible to assign too much intentionality to the effects of his lyrics, or even to the methods he employed that brought them into being. By all accounts he was withering, an extraordinarily shy person to force to make a pop record, even at his own acquiescence. For every occasional *I* on *Murmur* there are a dozen *me*s, where the real Stipe is being acted upon, a passive, object-like presence in his own song. Words are one thing, vocalizing another. He hid in the stairs under the control room in the dark with a mic, an umbilical cord in reverse, since he controlled it. By biographical comparison, even Kafka bought groceries occasionally and was spotted. Stipe ate only garlic, which loves the dark and keeps forever. His performances on *Murmur* are the outward gestures of an entity trying to hide himself from the world, from the terms of the world which nevertheless fascinated him, its vocabulary and its discourse, the people and actions in his own songs, landscapes into which he could finally retreat or even disappear, and in one sense, he failed. It must have been comforting. I'd know; I hid there as well sometimes, in the semi-dark, with Stipe's headphone feed. The feeling became so good and right it became something else entirely.

But Stipe was reborn from this purgatory of meaning and reference and the having to tell. Somewhere along the way he discovered it was not about pathology, but about strategy, a viable aesthetic strategy against the dystopia of the airwaves and the malls and the halls of cultural might, but still only one strategy among infinite possibilities. There was a blankness and a deep pause. Unlike a lot of memories, it was mostly sound.

NOTES

1. Michael Stipe once remarked, "People need to realize that there's a potential for a great deal of nonsense involved—that's a crucial element in pop songs." It's interesting to note the ways in which Stipe's conception of "nonsense" has changed over the course of twenty-odd years. Stipe would return to "rock and

roll"-sounding lyrics much later in R.E.M.'s career, around the time he also more-or-less deliberately lifted his self-imposed ban on the first-person. The "hey, hey, hey" refrain in 1991's "Radio Song" (from *Out of Time*) recalls the *hey hey*s from their teen anthem "Scheherezade," an unrecorded tune from circa 1980. This return is almost a rebuke to the new generation of indie rockers, like Pavement, who learned how to convolute the language of their lyrics from early R.E.M. albums—and from whom the band now had to distinguish themselves in an alt-radio landscape much more tolerant of "weird" lyricizing than was the case in 1983 when *Murmur* was released. Radio audiences that were stymied by *Murmur*'s obtuse vocals in 1983 now *expected* oblique lyricizing from the band; in fact, it was now part and parcel of R.E.M.'s identity.

2. In fact, as I mentioned in an earlier chapter, the change in R.E.M.'s live sound before and after *Murmur* is profound. It's as if hearing their own songs on long-playing vinyl gave them a kind of credence they'd been missing—live, they began to play the *Murmur* songs the way they sounded on the album.

APPENDIX[1]

Radio Free Europe

Beside yourself if radio's gonna stay
Reason it could polish up the gray
Put that put that put that up your wall
That this isn't country at all

Raving station
Beside yourself

Keep me out of country in the word
Deal the fortress leading us absurd
Push that push that push that to the hull
That this isn't nothing at all

Straight off the boat
Where to go?

Calling out in transit
Calling out in transit
Radio Free Europe
Radio

Beside defying media too fast
Instead of pushing palaces to fall
Put that put that put that before all
That this isn't fortunate at all

Radio station
Beside yourself

Calling out [on] in transit
Calling out [on] in transit
Radio Free Europe
Radio

Decide yourself
Calling on a boat
Media's too fast

Keep me out of country in the word
Disappointers into us absurd

Straight off the boat
Where to go?

Calling out in transit
Calling out in transit
Radio Free Europe
Radio Free Europe
Calling out in transit
Calling out in transit
Radio Free Europe
Radio Free Europe

Pilgrimage

[Take a turn / take a turn
Take our fortune / take our fortune]

They called the club a two-headed cow
Your hate clipped and distant
Your luck with pilgrimage
Rest assured this will not last
Take a turn for the worst
Your hate clipped and distant
Your luck a two-headed cow

Pilgrimage has gained momentum

Take a turn / take a turn
Take our fortune / take our fortune

You're speaking in tongues
It's worth a broken lip
Your hate clipped and distant
Your luck with pilgrimage
Rest assured this will not last
Take a turn for the worst
Your hate clipped and distant
Your luck a two-headed cow

The pilgrimage has gained momentum

Take a turn / take a turn
Take our fortune / take our fortune

Pilgrimage / Pilgrimage

Speaking in tongues
It's worth a broken lip
Your hate clipped and distant
Your luck
Rest assured this will not last
Take a turn for the worst
Your hate clipped and distant
Your luck / two-headed

Pilgrimage has gained momentum
Take a turn / take a turn
Take our fortune / take our fortune

Pilgrimage / Pilgrimage

Pilgrimage has gained momentum

Take a turn / take a turn
Take our fortune / take our fortune
Take a turn / take a turn
Take our fortune / take our fortune

Laughing

Laocoön and her two sons
Pressured storm tried to move
No other more emotion bound
Martyred misconstrued

Lighted
In a room / lanky room

Lighted lighted laughing in tune
Lighted lighted laughing

Laocoön and her two sons
Run the gamut sated view
Know them more emotion bound
Martyred misconstrued

Lighted
In a room / lanky room

Lighted lighted laughing in tune
Lighted lighted laughing

In a room
Lock the door
Latch the room

Lighted lighted laughing

Laocoön and her two sons
Ran the gamut settled new
Find a place fit to laugh
Lock the doors / latch the room

Lighted
In a room / lanky room

Lighted lighted laughing in tune
Lighted lighted laughing in tune
Lighted lighted laughing in tunes
Lighted lighted laughing in tune

Talk About the Passion

Empty prayer empty mouths combien reaction
Empty prayer empty mouths talk about the passion
Not everyone can carry the weight of the world
Not everyone can carry the weight of the world

Talk about the passion
Talk about the passion

Empty prayer empty mouths combien reaction
Empty prayer empty mouths talk about the passion

Combien
Combien
Combien du temps?

Talk about the passion
Talk about the passion

Not everyone can carry the weight of the world
Not everyone can carry the weight of the world

Combien
Combien
Combien du temps?

Talk about the passion
Talk about the passion
Talk about the passion
Talk about the passion
Talk about the passion
Talk about the passion
Talk about the passion

Moral Kiosk

Scratch the scandals in the twilight
Trying to shock but instead
Idle hands are Orient to her
Pass a magic pillow under head

So much more attractive
Inside the moral kiosk

Inside / cold / dark / fire / twilight
Inside / cold / dark / fire / twilight

Scratch the scandals in the twilight
She was laughing like a Horae
Put that knee in sour landslide
Take the steps to dash a roving eye

So much more attractive
Inside the moral kiosk

Inside / cold / dark / fire / twilight
Inside / cold / dark / fire / twilight

Scratch the scandals in the twilight
You're trying to shock but instead
Idle hands are Oriental head
Pass a magic pillow under head

So much more attractive
Inside the moral kiosk

Inside / cold / dark / fire / twilight
Inside / cold / dark / fire / twilight

[Fire . . .]

Inside / cold / dark / fire / twilight
Inside / cold / dark / fire / twilight

Perfect Circle

Put your hair back
We get to leave
Eleven gallows
On your sleeve
Shallow figure
Winners paid
Eleven shadows
Way out of place

Standing too soon shoulders high in the room
Standing too soon shoulders high in the room
Standing too soon shoulders high in the room

Pull your dress on
And stay real close

Who might leave you
Where I left off?
A perfect circle of
Acquaintances and friends
Drink another
Coin a phrase

Heaven assumed shoulders high in the room
Heaven assumed shoulders high in the room
Heaven assumed shoulders high in the room

Try to win and suit your needs
Speak out sometimes but try to win

Standing too soon shoulders high in the room
Standing too soon shoulders high in the room
Standing too soon shoulders high in the room
Standing too soon shoulders high in the room
Standing too soon shoulders high in the room

Catapult

Ooh we were little boys
Ooh we were little girls
It's nine o'clock don't try to turn it off
Cowered in a hole open your mouth to question

Did we miss anything?
Did we miss anything?
Did we miss anything?
Did we miss anything?

Catapult catapult
Catapult catapult

Ooh we were little boys
Ooh we were little girls

It's nine o'clock don't try to turn it off
Cowered in a hole open your mouth
We in step, in hand
Your mother remembers this
Hear the howl of the rope, a question

Did we miss anything?
Did we miss anything?
Did we miss anything?
Did we miss anything?

Catapult catapult
Catapult catapult

March could be darker
March could be darker

Catapult catapult
Catapult catapult

Ooh we were little boys
Ooh we were little girls

It's nine o'clock don't try to turn it off
Cowered in a hole open your mouth
We in step, in hand
Your mother remembers this
Hear the howl of the rope, a question

Did we miss anything?
Did we miss anything?
Did we miss anything?
Did we miss anything?

Catapult catapult
Catapult catapult
Catapult catapult

Sitting Still

This name I got we all agreed [were green]
See could stop stop it will red [well-read]
We could bind it in the scythe [combine it in a sense]
We could gather throw a fit

Up to par and Katie bar the kitchen signs but not me in
Setting trap [sit and try] for the big kill waste of time sitting still

I'm the sun and you can read
I'm the sun [sign] and you're not deaf
We could bind it in the scythe
We could gather throw a fit

Up to par and Katie bars the kitchen signs but not me in
Setting trap [sit and try] for the big kill waste of time sitting still

I can hear you
I can hear you
I can hear you

This name I got we all agreed
See could [secret] stop stop it will red [well-read]
We could bind it in the scythe [combine it in a sense]
We could gather throw a fit

Up to par and Katie bars the kitchen signs but not me in
Setting trap [sit and try] for the big kill waste of time sitting still

I can hear you
I can hear you
I can hear you

You can gather when I talk
Talk until you're blue
You could get away from me
Get away from me

*I'm up to par and [multiplying] Katie bars the kitchen signs but not
     me in
Sit and try for the big kill a waste of time sitting still*

*I can hear you
I can hear you
I can hear you*

*I can hear you
I can hear you
I can hear you
Can you hear me?*

9 – 9

*[Steady repetition is a compulsion mutually reinforced
Now what does that mean?
Is there a just contradiction?
Nothing much
Now I lay me down to sleep I pray the Lord my soul to keep
If I should die before I wake I pray the Lord hesitate]*

*Got to punch
Right on target
Twisting tongues
Gotta stripe
Down his back
All nine yards
Down her back*

*Give me a couple
Don't give me a couple of
Pointers turn to lies and
Conversation fear*

Got to punch
Right on target
Twisting tongues
Gotta stripe
Down his back
All nine yards
Down her back

Give me a couple
Don't give me a couple of
Pointers turn to lies and
Conversation

What is in my mind?
What is in my mind?

[Steady repetition is a compulsion mutually reinforced
Now what does that mean?
Is there a just contradiction?
Nothing much
Now I lay me down to sleep I pray the Lord my soul to keep
If I should die before I wake I pray the Lord hesitate hesitate]

Got to punch
Right on target
Twisting's done
Gotta stripe
Down her back
All nine yards
Down his back

Give me a couple
Don't give me a couple of
Pointers turn to lies and
Conversation fear

To conversation fear
Conversation fear
Conversation fear

Shaking Through

Could it be that one small voice
Doesn't count in the room?
Yellow like a geisha gown
Denying all the way

Could this by three be ten?
Order marches on
Yellow like a geisha gown
Denial all the way

Shaking through
Opportune
Shaking through
Opportune

Are we grown way too far?
Taking after rain
Yellow like a geisha gown
Denying all the way

Shaking through
Opportune
Shaking through
Opportune

In my life

Ears that are still
Children of today on parade

Yellow like a geisha gown
Denying all the way

Shaking through
Opportune
Shaking through
Opportune

Shaking through
Opportune
Shaking through
Opportune

We Walk

Up the stairs to the landing
Up the stairs into the hall
Take oasis
Marat's bathing

We walk through the wood
We walk

Up the stairs to the landing
Up the stairs into the hall
Take oasis
Marat's bathing

We walk through the woods
We walk

Take oasis / take oasis / take oasis / take oasis

Up the stairs to the landing
Up the stairs into the hall
Take oasis
Marat's bathing

We walk through the world
We walk

Up the stairs to the landing
Up the stairs into the hall
Take oasis
Marat's bathing
Up the stairs to the landing
Up the stairs into the hall
Take oasis
Marat's bathing
Up the stairs to the landing
Up the stairs into the hall
Into the
Into up
Up / up
Up / up / up / up
Up / up / up / up
Up / up / up

West of the Fields

Long gone intuition
To assume are gone
When we try

Dream of living jungle
In my way back home
When we die

West of the fields
West of the fields
West of the fields
West of the fields

Long gone / long gone / long gone / long gone
West of the fields

Dreams of Elysian
To assume are gone
When we try

Tell now what is dreaming
When we try to listen with your eyes
Oversimplify

West of the fields
West of the fields
West of the fields
West of the fields
Long gone / long gone / long gone / long gone
West of the fields

The animals
How strange [have strayed]
Try try this trick [. . .]
The animals
How strange
Try try this trick at hand

Dreams of Elysian
To assume are gone
When we try
Tell now what is dreaming
When we try
Listen with your eyes
When we die

West of the fields
West of the fields
West of the fields
West of the fields

Long gone / long gone / long gone / long gone
West of the fields

West of the fields
West of the fields
West of the fields
West of the fields
Long gone / long gone / long gone / long gone
West of the fields

NOTES

1. Some of these lyrics were derived by triangulating the album's songs against early live versions and demos. Many thanks again to Mitch Easter, for retrieving Michael Stipe's handwritten lyric sheet to "Radio Free Europe" from his studio's tape vault.

Also available in the series

ALSO AVAILABLE IN THE SERIES

ALSO AVAILABLE IN THE SERIES